Conversations on/for South Asia

Debating the Ancient and Present

A Conversation with Romila Thapar

Conversations on/for South Asia Series Editors:

Sasanka Perera
Ravi Kumar
Dev Pathak

Bio-note on the editor:

Sasanka Perera is Professor and the Dean of the Faculty of Social Sciences at South Asian University, New Delhi. After completing his PhD in Cultural Anthropology from University of California, Santa Barbara in 1991, he served the Department of Sociology at University of Colombo, Sri Lanka for 19 years. He was the Head of Sociology at Colombo University at the time of his resignation in 2011. His research interests include contemporary social theory with an emphasis on the idea of visual culture and its politics, urban space, politics of nationalism, religion and ethnicity. His academic interests have enabled him to work in Sri Lanka, USA, Cambodia, Pakistan, Nepal, Japan and India. He has written extensively and published in Sri Lanka and internationally in the English and Sinhala languages while some of his work has also been published in Tamil, Japanese and Spanish. He was the Editor in Chief of *South Asia Journal for Culture* from 2008 to 2012 and now edits *Society and Culture in South Asia*, co-published by Sage and South Asian University.

Conversations on/for South Asia

Debating the Ancient and Present

A Conversation with Romila Thapar

Edited by

Sasanka Perera

SAU
SOUTH ASIAN UNIVERSITY
Sociology@SAU

AAKAR

DEBATING THE ANCIENT AND PRESENT
A Conversation with Romila Thapar

Edited by Sasanka Perera

First Published 2015

Reprinted 2017

ISBN 978-93-5002-336-5

Published by
AAKAR BOOKS
28 E Pocket IV, Mayur Vihar Phase I, Delhi 110 091
Phone : 011 2279 5505 Telefax : 011 2279 5641
aakarbooks@gmail.com; www.aakarbooks.com

In association with
Department of Sociology
Faculty of Social Sciences
South Asian University
Akbar Bhavan, Chanakyapuri,
New Delhi 110 021, India
Email: sociology@soc.sau.ac.in

Printed at
Sapra Brothers, Delhi 110 092

Contents

Series Note

Conversations on/for South Asia

The Department of Sociology at South Asian University was established in 2011 within the Faculty of Social Sciences. In defining its vision and approach to teaching and research, the Department of Sociology notes on its website that it is "acutely aware of the non-existence of regular and serious forums for South Asian scholarship in social sciences to showcase our own research and thinking." This series is an effort on the part of the Department to create a platform of critical knowledge on issues that have been vital to South Asia.

As a series, *Conversations on/for South Asia* intends to keep itself open-ended, more so keeping in mind the necessity of inventing and re-inventing scholarship in and around ever dynamic South Asian societies. The series would not only publish conversations with South Asian scholars on vital issues of concern but would also be open to publishing other kinds of texts that contribute to a critical understanding of the region whose definition, intellectually, is mired in numerous debates and anxieties. It is one of the textual tools through which the Department of Sociology hopes to expand its thinking to the wider public domain in South Asia and the world in addition to its journal, *Society and Culture in South Asia*.

Each instalment in the series will be published under the editorial responsibility of one of the series editors.

Preface and Acknowledgements

'Debating the Ancient and Present,' an interactive workshop with Professor Romila Thapar moderated and chaired by Professor Rustom Bharucha was held on August 22, 2013 at the South Asian University under the auspices of the Department of Sociology and the Faculty of Social Sciences.

In its published form, 'Debating the Ancient and Present: A Conversation with Romila Thapar' is the first instalment in the publication series, *Conversations on/for South Asia'* launched by the Department of Sociology at South Asian University in 2015.

In the initial planning stage of the intellectual encounter with Professor Romila Thapar, we invited her for a lecture in the conventional sense as part of the 'Exploring South Asia' series initiated by the Faculty of Social Sciences. However, she rightly suggested an alternative and more interactive format where a conversation could take place based on pertinent issues on the politics of history-writing as well as seeing the past. In the long term, this format has since then been fine-tuned as one of the main intellectual outreach approaches of the Department of Sociology.

Under the ambit of 'Exploring South Asia,' we invited a wide-range of individuals with an interest in ideas of history, past and the politics of historiography to send in their questions based on their readings of a number of Professor Thapar's well-known texts which include the following: *Early India: From The Origin to 1300 AD* (2004); *2001. Cultural Pasts: Essays in Early Indian History* (2001) *and Somanatha: The Many Voices of a History* (2005).

The questions generated in this manner as well as others

that emerged from the floor at the time created the basic foundation for the conversation. As we know, Professor Thapar's work primarily focuses on Indian history. It is her engrossed engagement with this 'past' which also constituted the conversation at our university. However, it is also clear that the larger issues which emerge in unravelling the Indian past and the manner in which the writing of that past gets entangled in the politics of the present has equal relevance to the rest of South Asia. In the politics of our region, the past is never too far from the present where it is constantly revisited, reinvented and refashioned, in some cases to such an extent that the difference between historiography and creative writing becomes blurred. In that sense, the competitive understandings of the past is often an emotional and ideological battleground in the present.

In making this event possible, I would like to acknowledge the tireless work my colleague Dev Nath Pathak as coordinator of the event along with his team put in. In the same spirit, I would also like to thank my friend and colleague Rustom Bharucha from the School of Arts and Aesthetics at Jawaharlal Nehru University for agreeing to chair and moderate the session, which brought his enormous experience in his own inimitable style to bear upon the conversation. I am very grateful to Professor Thapar for taking considerable time from her busy schedule to carefully edit and fine-tune her text. I also acknowledge the creative efforts of Anoli Perera in designing the cover for the present instalment as well as for the series.

In formulating the text for publishing, we have edited it minimally, keeping the spirit, the feel and the nuances of the conversation intact.

Sasanka Perera

Professor and Dean
Faculty of Social Sciences
South Asian University
New Delhi

April 6, 2015

Introductions

What follows are the proceedings of a conversation with Professor Romila Thapar organized by the Faculty of Social Sciences and the Department of Sociology at South Asian University as part of the 'Exploring South Asia Lecture Series' on August 22, 2013 at FSI Hall, South Asian University, New Delhi.

*****

Sasanka Perera: This is one of those moments that is worth a celebration. I would ideally like to get straight into the conversation. But then, as a formal institution we also have ritual obligations to perform. So can I ask the President of the University, Professor Chadha to formally welcome the guests today by offering these two bouquets of flowers to them please? Today my life has been made easy, my work has been made easy because we have a fairly committed group of competent colleagues and students who can visualize things well and do the necessary hard work to make sure that the kind of things we envisage such as today's' conversation move beyond our dreams into the realm of reality.

Personally I'm very happy that after a very long time we have two of my favourite writers in this room—Professor Romila Thapar as well as Professor Rustom Bharucha. Why do I say this? Because the first time I read something by Professor Thapar was not in English, it was in my own language—Sinhala. Today, I find it quite significant that the only reason I could read it at the time was because it was available to me in my own language. My wife had read it for her A-level class in history as well. I can't remember who translated it. But I think it was *A History of India,* which at that time was part of the A-level history syllabus for Sri Lanka. But in some bizarre moment of 'wisdom' that I cannot fathom, that text has been now removed from the syllabus along with Indian history. The second time I read about her was also in Sinhala. That was the kind of essay that got Professor Thapar and many other Indian historians into much trouble in the recent past. I am referring to an essay co-written by her, Bipan Chandra and Harbans Mukhia about the writing of Indian history, looking at textbooks. These were my initial introductions to Professor Thapar. When I was talking to my students much later as a university teacher, for me she epitomized the kind of person who was worth emulating as a scholar and as a kind of public intellectual who intervened socially at crucial moments in the evolution of recent history.

On the other hand, it was much later that I read Professor Bharucha; first I think it was *The Politics of Cultural Practice* that I read a long time ago when I picked up the book at the Book Worm during one of my many visits to Delhi. Then much more recently—I don't know if this is his latest book—the book that I enjoyed the most was *Another Asia.* And I was wondering how it is possible for someone to talk about serious intellectual matters in a language that was bordering on poetry as well as erudite fiction all at the same time. I was always quite envious of him because most of us can come nowhere near that kind of writing. So this is why it is very good to have both these scholars with us today. The formal introductions will be done by my colleague, Dev Pathak, who is the coordinator of this event.

I just want to rattle off a few things to get this conversation going. For me, and for most of you I suppose, history is really not something of the past alone. It has to do with the present too. In day-to-day life and politics, the way in which we look at the past has really nothing much to do with what actually happened at a particular moment. This is what the actuality of historiography will anyway tell us. In the very least, you will have multiple versions, narratives talking about the past. So then, at some point one will have to deal with the questions, what is actual fact? What is not? Who is silenced and who is heard and so on. Is valid evidence available to make a specific historical claim or are such claims made simply on the basis of hearsay or emotionally charged mythic narratives? I am sure many of these issues will come up in the conversation that would follow.

It is in such contexts that the idea of the so-called "fear of history" might come up. I was wondering why South Asian University doesn't have a history department or teaching of history as part of its planning. I wonder whether it is also related to the fact that histories often need to be authenticated by somebody in power the way it often happens in our part of the world. So when you're looking at the University that is South Asian in the sense of its governance, then who has the power to authorize a particular kind of history? But that doesn't mean that those of us who teach in the Faculty of Social Sciences—in today's context we have two departments—are not free to smuggle in histories. But they have to be smuggled in. After all, none of the things that we teach can be done out of context of history, which is why we have invited, among other things, Professor Thapar to be with us today.

Let me make a few more comments about the series; we call this 'Exploring South Asia'. It was started in 2012 as an ongoing series for the Faculty of Social Sciences. It is open to any colleague who wants to invite somebody to look at some aspect of South Asian politics, culture and so on and so forth. In 2012, we started off with a lecture on the politics of doing archaeology by Professor Sudarshan Seneviratne from Sri Lanka and accidentally or incidentally he is also one of the first students of JNU trained by Professor Thapar. Then we have today's conversation, and on the 26th we have a talk under the same series by Iftikhar Dadi from Cornell University. He will talk to us about contemporary art in Pakistan and how art negotiates with politics. The reason for setting up the series was because even though we work in a place called South Asian University, we are really not sure what South Asia actually means—South Asian or South Asia as a collective identity. You have fairly unsure borders; you already know what is happening in India's borders and we have a very difficult time going from one place to another within this geo-political entity, but at the same time we have—particularly as a Department and also as a Faculty—

often wondered if it isn't possible to imagine South Asia far more inclusively and imaginatively than it is done today? Particularly the thinking by entities like SAARC on this matter seems to be in black and white which never really works like this on the ground.

Let me end, with a note on why we are here in this place called South Asian University. For me, it is a matter of making and writing our own intellectual and institutional history. We're also not here to emulate any other institution beyond a point. We will of course borrow ideas and personnel from the great institutions in this city as well as in the region. But we are not here to emulate either Delhi University or JNU in the real sense of the word. We are here to set up our own institution and the only way we can do that is to make sure that the University becomes a centre for serious and sustained intellectual activity in which people outside the University can also take part. That is why all the activities organized by the Faculty of Social Sciences—like our seminars and this conversation—are open to the public. So I hope at least some of you will continue to come to our activities as we go on. I don't want to take any further time; I think I have said what I wanted to say, and I would like to invite Dev to come and introduce the speakers and then we can go on with it. Thank you very much.

Dev Pathak: Thank you Sasanka. By way of contextualizing this workshop and to briefly introduce our guests, I will be just reading out though it's not a very interesting task to do it this way. But it will save time. So to contextualize it, we can say that historiography, as it emerges from the discourses of philosophy, is not merely about the craft, method and the technique of narrating a chronologically informed account. In terms of wider implications, it is also about a valued orientation towards the art of interpretation and understanding. This is the fundamental underpinning of the workshop today. Art subsumes a unique rational structure which is not devoid of creative paradoxes. This is perhaps why it gives birth to polyphony of meaning by engaging with multiple texts and contexts. Does it mean however that there is a history of fragments and a history of a national whole and these shall never meet? Does it mean that a

Dalit history, a Hindu history of *Aryavart*, a history of man and another history of women are small islands separated by accidents in history writing?

It is in this context that this workshop is pregnant with possibilities for all of us who seek to maintain a possible infinity in the art of interpretation and understanding despite the ever-ready opposition from society and polity to the free spirit of enquiry. Lastly, this workshop is also an attempt to bridge the gaps between humanities, arts and social sciences in the historical milieu which forcefully compels social science to be a-historical and a-philosophical. This is to prevent the mishap that plagued natural sciences long ago. This workshop is a fruit of an insistence by Professor Romila Thapar on the idea of interactive deliberation when we requested her for a lecture. It shows her preference for dialogue over monologue. What else can signify a seasoned teacher of history? We welcome her with a deep sense of gratitude here today. It is a difficult task to introduce Professor Thapar, too magnanimous a phenomenon in South Asian academia to be satisfactorily introduced in a few words. One can mention her illustrious presence in the domain of Indian academics for over six decades as an ever enthusiastic teacher, as a prolific writer of monographs and as a lucid essayist and most importantly, as a public intellectual who is ever willing to sign a memorandum of protest on the issues of pitching concern.

One can say that she began to teach at the University of Delhi in 1963 and joined Jawaharlal Nehru University in 1970. One can mention some of her seminal works from amidst numerous such texts as *Asoka and the Decline of the Mauryas; A History of India; Sakuntala: Texts, Readings, Histories; History and Beyond; Cultural Pasts: Essays in Early Indian History; Early India; Somanatha: The Many Voices of a History* and of course the beautifully written NCERT textbooks—my personal choice—*Ancient India* and *Medieval India*. This listing too, however, would leave somebody like me ungratified.

Even so, can it be enough to mention the academic distinctions that have been bestowed upon her all over the world such as Visiting Professorship at Cornell University, Fellow at SOAS, University of London, at Peradeniya University, Sri

Lanka, at University of Chicago or her laurels such as Fukuoka Asian Cultural Prize, Presidentship of the Indian History Congress, Honorary D.Litts at Calcutta, Oxford, Edinburgh and so on and so forth. A long list of achievements of Professor Thapar will not exhaust the interests of a seeker like myself.

However, a fragment of a personal narrative could help mark the beginning for an engagement with her works. It comes from one of my friends who was doing history at JNU while I was enrolled in the Sociology programme. I once chatted with him saying that there are no more luminaries in the Centre for Historical Studies at JNU to guide young intellectuals. He came back with a disarming repartee when he observed: "They are still there. I experienced Romila Thapar speaking to me even in my personal domain." This is the legend of a scholar in campus folklore providing inspiration for not only students but also young teachers of my generation. Professor Thapar is also a legend in the history of historical studies in India and hence, at the gunpoint of intolerant politics while commanding an immense amount of respect all over the world.

Moving on, the chair of the workshop is one of the most renowned scholars who has been able to construct a much-needed bridge between performance studies and social sciences. Professor Rustom Bharucha, after being a freelance director, dramatist, prolific thinker and writer for twenty-five years is now a Professor at the School of Arts and Aesthetics, JNU. He was awarded a Japan Foundation Fellowship, for his stunning work on Tagore and Okakura. Befitting the enormity of his achievements are some of his internationally acclaimed monographs such as *Rehearsals of Revolutions: The Political Theatre of Bengal; Theatre and the World: Performance and the Politics of Culture; In the Name of the Secular: Contemporary Cultural Activism in India; Another Asia: Rabindranath Tagore and Okakura Tenshin; The Politics of Cultural Practice: Thinking Through Theatre in an Age of Globalization*—this was nominated as an outstanding title by the 'Choice' in 2011. Not least in importance is his piece titled *The Question of Faith* in the 'Tracts for the Times' series edited by S. Gopal and Romila Thapar and also his contribution in *India: Another Millennium?* edited by Romila Thapar.

Quite in tandem with the manifested scholarship of

Professor Bharucha, Javed Malik once identified him as one of the few writers who through their writings have tried to raise the standard of theatre scholarship in India. Similarly, most significant is a comment by one of the American anthropologists of theatre, Professor John Emig, who said in a personal communication—"Rustom unsettles the comfort zone of the Western dramaturgy by bringing in politics in the domain of performance."

Given the presence of illuminating scholars such as Professor Thapar and Professor Bharucha, the call for this workshop received an enthusiastic response from young scholars and teachers from institutions based in Delhi. It only indicated as to how history is indeed "a very contemporary interest". In the presence of the capable chair of the workshop, we envisage an enriching and enlivening interaction with Professor Thapar. May I now request Professor Bharucha to kindly commence the workshop. Thank you.

The Conversation

Image courtesy of South Asian University Archive.

Rustom Bharucha: Thanks Dev and thank you everybody for coming. It's indeed a very great honour for me to accept this invitation to chair what is being called an interactive workshop session and that's what Professor Thapar has opted for. As we know, Professor Thapar is one of the most revered historians in India. So when I was asked to speak here, I felt a bit reluctant. I felt it was a bit presumptuous on my part to accept the role of the chair, not because Professor Thapar is a great scholar but more precisely because she's a great historian, and history is not my discipline as Dev pointed out. So how could I presume to chair something like this? The only history that I have written is an oral history of Rajasthan which was drawn out of conversations with Komal Kothari, a very great human being whom I think Romila has a deep regard for. Komal da had this extraordinary knowledge of marginalized communities living in the dessert, their material culture, their practices, and he interacted with them for fifty years. That was something quite extraordinary.

I remember meeting Professor Thapar at that time, sharing my diffidence because I was not an oral historian, and I was not a Rajasthani specialist. And she said, well maybe precisely because you're not a specialist, maybe you are the right person for this particular job. Objectively, I think she was saying something accurate because if I had been a specialist, frankly, I would have stopped him quite so often when he was talking to me for eight hours on end. He had that epic sense of time. And I would have stopped him and I would ask him to contextualize this and verify this and the flow of his knowledge, cutting across many different contexts of land, water, irrigation, livestock, ritual practices, shrines, *sati, Teratali, Pabuji,* etc as well as his work on music. However, I don't believe that I can use that rationale of what I would call "strategic non-expertise" to apply to this particular conversation for the simple reason that the context is different and Romila Thapar is an academic, Komal Kothari was not an academic. As Dev has pointed out, Professor Thapar is steeped, not just in her own writing, but in the shaping and in the formation of history as a discipline in post-independence India. The shaping of a discipline and the investment that goes into it, the struggle that goes into it, and the commitment that goes into it, is something very very specific. And yes, in that context I do feel a little diffident. However, this lack will be more than compensated by the eighteen speakers with specific questions from the audience who are lined up, and I think from being the centre of attention, you may very well become the proverbial calm in the eye of the storm because you never know what to expect in a workshop.

Okay, so we're here to debate the ancient and the present. This is quite broad. I would like to contextualize that with a lecture I first heard Professor Thapar giving at JNU long ago when I had not the slightest inkling that I would be teaching there. She was lecturing on time, on ancient Indian concepts of time which later got formulated in that remarkable book—my favourite—*Time as a Metaphor of History.* History as a metaphor of time one could say. An extraordinary reflection. We all know there's a very deep, complex relationship between the dynamics that exist between history and time; but to examine those dynamics through the mediation of metaphor is quite special.

Historians are not known to be particularly drawn to metaphors; they're suspicious of metaphors at times. Indeed Komal Kothari was intensely suspicious of metaphors. He didn't know how to deal with them. Metaphor is basically a literary category, and to examine the concept of history and time through the mediation of metaphor is really some kind of a coup. It makes me think of Hannah Arendt in her *Eight Exercises in Political Thought,* in a remarkable book called *Between Past and Future.* In that introduction, she basically says metaphors are useful not because they tell us what to think, but how to think, and the 'how' is very important in Romila Thapar's work, and we're going to get to that soon enough.

Now, I'm bringing this up for a very specific reason relating to the topic here, the debate here. In that lecture, in ancient Indian concepts of time as I remember it, Professor Thapar did not make one explicit reference to the turbulent present, the turbulent political present then and indeed now. Not one. But, and this is the interesting point, there was no doubt in my mind and there was no doubt in the minds of the people there that she was indeed engaging with the most political immediacies of a very messy and complicated present post-December 6, 1992. I found that fascinating and rare. How is it possible to make you think about something in the present when you're not actually addressing it? I found that very very unusual.

As a performance theorist, I would say what we had there was some kind of a very carefully crafted, intentional, discursive speech act. It was not accidental; it was very powerful. Now let me make it clear, this is not the only way in which an intervention can be made. There are times when, as we will be talking about, you will have to confront things more directly. You will not be able to work through subtlety, erasure, evasion, allusion or whatever. You'll have to take the question head on, and she has done that and we'll talk about that, but that's not the only way to work. Public intellectualism is one intervention but it's not the only intervention. What I admired about that lecture is that you can be stringently scholarly and yet the political can resonate. Politics is not the prerogative of public intellectuals alone, not at all. Scholars can also make the political resonate in more complex ways. In a more concrete way, there's obviously something about the content of the concepts that she was talking about that had this capacity to resonate the present. And that is something very humbling for all of us that these ancient Indian concepts going back centuries, how are they resonate today? We may not know the terms, we may not know those categories; but the principles underlying those concepts are being invoked, they're being appropriated, they're being distorted, they're being invented, they're being mythologized and they are being communalized.

That span where you can read the present through the ancient makes me think that when you just look at the wording of the encounter today—debating the ancient and the present—the ancient and the present are seen as to separate categories which are connected through a conjunction. I think we're actually living in something like the "ancient present" and that's what makes me very moved by where we live in India—the "ancient present".

Now getting to the issue of the ancient Romila, I'm going to come to the first question to kick off this discussion. You've invested in the ancient for the longest time. It's a vexed category. We don't really use this word "ancient" in everyday life except ironically I think. So it gets sometimes annexed to a very "singularized" reading of history. It often gets linked to ancient India as opposed to your very wonderful title—early India. So what's the difference between ancient and early you might say. There's a shift. For me, early opens something out, I'm speaking from my point of view. Ancient kind of gets it closed. There's a baggage, there's a closure there, there's a certain weight. It's a normative category; we know it's convenient etc. But there's a weight there, it's vexed. So I would like you to just kick off the discussion by saying what are some of the traps in engaging with the ancient? And what are some of the strategies that you have come across, which you've developed for yourself in dealing with these traps? So may I ask you just to start then?

Romila Thapar: I'd like to begin by saying that I'm delighted to have this invitation to come here. I think as one grows older, one really does look forward very much to the opportunity to meet and talk with new people, so I am greatly looking forward to this afternoon. This is an occasion when one expects a continuation of provocative questions. So thank you very much for the invitation and also for all the very complimentary things that you have said. Yes, I opted for a question-answer session because I thought giving a lecture would be in some ways too static. You'd all be sitting here, I'd walk in, there'd be a little introduction, I'd pull out my twenty pages, and I would read them out, three or four of you would ask three or four questions, and I'd walk out. I thought it would be more interesting perhaps if we could have a little 'to-ing' and 'fro-ing.' So I'm glad that that was conceded.

Now to turn to the question as to why ancient and what's early. Yes, I started studying ancient history very seriously as "ancient Indian history", trained for it, and was quite happy doing that without second thoughts until after my training and my PhD in London. I came back to India and started teaching "ancient Indian history". Then slowly and gradually I began to realize that one aspect of what I was teaching was really an aspect of present-day India. The connection that Rustom was making between the ancient and the present is a very deep connection. It refers at one level to attempts we make in tracing rituals or performances of music and dance back to three thousand years ago, and which we're still performing. But these don't really matter too much except to those involved.

Image courtesy of South Asian University Archive

I'm talking about something else that is almost—one doesn't know quite how to express it—intangible. You can't hear it, or see it, but somehow it's there. There's something about the present which goes back into the past. In a sense, over the years, I gradually realized—as Rustom said—that if you use the term "ancient" you're carrying the baggage of historiography with you. Ancient—how did it come about? The first modern writing of Indian history was by James Mill who divided it into three periods: the "Hindu civilization", followed by the "Muslim civilization", followed by the British. Please remember that when we talk about the "Hindu" period and the "Muslim" period, we're not making distinctions made by Indians. We're making distinctions made by a colonial policy, and that was one reason why many of us in the 1960s, discarded these terms. But before that, they had also been discarded by certain nationalist historians who said, "no" to Hindu, Muslim, and British periods as these categories were too communal; this periodization is based on the religion of the rulers so it doesn't describe what was necessarily important to the rest of society. They switched to "ancient, medieval and modern", because European history was also being discussed in terms of ancient Europe, medieval Europe and modern Europe. But what they didn't do was to find fresh ways of demarcating the periods. Where were the time-lines to be drawn? Where does the ancient period end and the medieval period begin? So they retained the terminal points of the old periodization and it remained exactly the same. The ancient period was the Hindu period, it ended in 1000 AD and then came the Muslim period which was called the medieval period which ended in 1757 at the Battle of Plassey, and then came the modern period which is the British period. So in effect we were back with our little boxes, carefully controlled, strictly determined.

For a long time, one went on living with these boxes, teaching through these boxes because it was convenient. Every time I would suggest to my colleagues in JNU that we might drop these titles because the course we were teaching was a lengthier course or a shorter course, and they would say that it's convenience lies in students being familiar with it and they will know what they're going to be reading about. The other problem was that jobs were and still are, advertised keeping these three specializations in mind so a student not having one of these labels would lose out on getting jobs. Okay, but after some years of that I began to say to myself—this is not on. I'm not going to remain stuck in this boxed-code, "ancient" because I see a certain continuity not only from the ancient into the medieval, but in some cases all along the line into the present. This sense of the past being tied into the present is quite subtle which perhaps we still have to discover. I don't know that we've discovered it yet. We know that it's there; there's evidence for it being there in monuments and excavated artefacts, but that very subtle subterranean channel as it were, that connects the ancient to the present, that is something that we haven't really fully explored.

So I thought about it at great length, and I thought what should one replace it with? And then I thought obviously, there is a beginning and that's the early period. It's when things are moving around, grappling with creating ideas, not knowing which way they're going, and then slowly taking shape and form. And what am I doing? I'm looking at this process of change and reformulation that is going on through the centuries to the present. Therefore, I thought "early" is the more efficient way of describing this. Not only the continuity, but also—as you said Rustom—the fact that early has loose ends. You don't have to define that early begins at this point because there's always an earlier beginning. Wherever you begin, there's an earlier beginning. So you leave it vague and you can't say that "early" ends at this point because who knows? A particular form of the early may have ended earlier, but there may be another that carries on later and ends later and the historian has to see it through and notice if it undergoes changes. So there's a kind of nice vagueness about the use of the term "early" which allows one to be flexible about beginnings and endings. The historical context becomes as important as the transit through time, if not a trifle more important.

There was another reason too that I found as I started doing research that the most artificial thing about Indian history is precisely this periodization of ancient, medieval and modern. Why? Because the tradition has always been that for the

"Hindu" period or the ancient period or whatever you choose to call it, you use Sanskrit sources. When you come to the medieval period, you switch to Persian sources. I began to see that for example, if you were working on the history of something from 1000 AD to 1500 AD, very often and interestingly views diverse from Persian sources, were expressed in Sanskrit sources and in the regional language sources because they were giving a different perspective. In my research, I started moving forward and using these sources rather than stopping at AD 1000 and feeling that I have to switch to Persian. So the advantage of "early" was again that one could happily move on, take one's categories of sources along with one into the medieval period as well—as I did—for example, in the study of *Somanatha*. It was not that I used any new sources to contest the received opinion about Mahmud of Ghazni's raid on the temple at Somanatha. I used only the well-known much-used published sources, so there was nothing new about the sources. But I did not stop with the Sanskrit sources at 1000 AD. I carried on till they carried on and then saw what they have to say. So in that way, it's been really a shift from a well-defined period with a beginning and an end as it were, to something that is much more flexible.

Rustom Bharucha: Thanks Romila. That's a very lucid answer. Let's kick off the session getting the audience involved. As a theatre person, the most important thing is that you have to begin by acknowledging where you are. If you're here you're here, you're not somewhere else. So I'm going to ask Dev, is Dev around here? Dev may I ask you to kick off the debate with the first question which actually has to deal with the location of this debate in the context of the South Asian University and indeed of Asia in general.

Dev Pathak: This was pre-empted, and Sasanka mentioned as to how history can be reconfigured in the larger context of South Asia primarily because we know what is called history, in India, would probably not be called history in Pakistan and what is called history in Pakistan would probably not be called history in Bangladesh. Therefore many cultural anthropologists have argued that when these countries of South Asia have to talk about their history, all they have to say is what is not their history. So they have to approach it negatively rather than positively. I dared asking this question precisely because I remembered your visualization of South Asia at the launch of the newly redesigned *Himal South Asian*, and that was an illuminating visualization we, in anthropology, would like to celebrate. But how do we celebrate, especially when we are faced with this fractured notion of history when it comes to different country contexts of South Asia?

Romila Thapar: Yes, let me start by saying that I have a suggestion for a project in your university. I think that you should not start with a history department. Why don't you start by organizing a workshop of South Asian historians to discuss the question of whether there can be a South Asian history and if so how to proceed to write it? I think it might be great fun and intellectually most challenging. You would have historians from Pakistan saying, their history starts in the 8th century AD with the conquest of Sind and you would have historians from India saying, 'well what about the Harappans? How do you fit in that culture?' Then you'd have historians from Bhutan perhaps saying that history for them starts with the arrival of Buddhism in Bhutan and then someone else would ask what was there prior to that. Buddhism didn't arrive into a vacuum. So the attempt is not to find linear similarities between one place and another. You can't say that if there was proto-historic culture in one part of the subcontinent, it must happen everywhere. No, it happens at different times in different places and sometimes altogether differently. So then, the important question becomes why does it happen at different times which leads you to very fundamental questions that all historians do ask and should ask, which is, what leads to the evolution of a particular culture, society and its history? How does it begin or how does it get formed? Does it come after a break or maybe after quiescence or whatever. But this is a basic question.

This textbook that you were referring to which was published in 1964—*Ancient India* for Middle School—I wrote it from a nationalist perspective. I was writing the history of the nation-state of India, and therefore, was trying to bring in, tuck into this history, all that was going on in the different parts of what was constituted as the nation-state of India and a little beyond that in fact. I was attacked for this by "liberal" historians who said I was being statist by taking the identity of the nation as a kind of background, although I was not arguing that this identity was prior to modern times and that it went back to the past. I kept trying to argue that this was not an attempt to be statist.

This was an attempt to say that everybody that belongs to this nation has a history and how does it correlate with the history of the neighbouring region. That's really a basic question in the history of a larger area. How do you correlate the history of one region with the history of the region that is juxtaposed to it? I think the importance of this is really what historians are now recognizing, and that is the usefulness of comparative history; that you cannot focus on one region alone without considering what was happening right around it—and making comparisons with what was happening where. Again the same question comes up all the time. Why? Why is there a difference? And you have to explain the difference and in terms of explaining the difference, you begin to understand, a little more I think, the history of the region that you're working on. So if we were to ask questions of our neighbours as to why their history is different, we would begin to understand much more about Indian history as well.

That was part of what I was talking about at the *Himal South Asian* launch in addressing the question of boundaries. Today boundaries are so rigid and so sacrosanct, and what I was saying was that the essence of a boundary, if you look at it historically, is that it was earlier virtually non-existent in the present sense because it was notional. These were imagined barriers, imagined differences.

In the Mauryan period for example, what was a boundary? It was a mountain, a river, a forest, a desert or the sea. It was some environmental feature which differentiated region A from region B, and it was really a frontier zone, but we treat it as a boundary. The inscriptions of Ashoka, the Mauryan emperor, are plotted on a map and it is said this was the extent of the

Mauryan Empire. I have problems with this because how do we know that the in-between regions were under Mauryan control? They need not have been. It could have been a system where people established themselves in different parts of a region, without necessarily controlling it in entirety, uniformly and unilaterally. I was also arguing that the notions of boundaries change with the use of cartography because then there is a map of the region and lines can be drawn to demarcate territory. So the line becomes very important in the politics of today. If you go back through the history of the Indian subcontinent, we're full of lines. There was the Durand Line, the McMahon line and in six weeks I believe, Brigadier Ross drew a partition line between what became India and Pakistan. In some ways such lines are an absurdity, although central to current international politics. The territory of two nation-states is created by taking a pencil and drawing it across a map and allotting villages to one or the other on the basis of the religion of the majority populations inhabiting each. How many members of this community live in this village and how many of that community in other villages?

This is not the way in which boundaries work. Human boundaries work in a different fashion and if you're drawing boundaries on a map, I would suggest that human boundaries be consulted as well. Therefore, I was trying to argue that this is a very complex word—boundary. What does it actually mean? It doesn't have the meaning that we often simplistically give it. It is not a simple matter of dividing one nation-state from another and leaving it at that.

Rustom Bharucha: All these boundaries, the absence of fluidity all over. That's always the case. Things get more rigid, more defined and in some ways more insensitive to human needs and concerns. Human beings are not consulted; they're just being represented. It's assumed that they will belong here and not there. Okay, I'm going to club together three questions and they're all on early India. There are three of you who have posed questions. There's Novojit Sen from the Department of History in the University of Delhi; there's Sojendra Mukherjee, also from the Department of History, University of Delhi and Baisakhi

Sengupta—where's Baisakhi? Hi Baisakhi—from the Centre for Historical Studies at JNU. All Bengali and all are talking about early India. So in the spirit of the debate—your questions are quite elaborate, just get to the point.

Novojit Sen: Do the boundaries, do they not only function in terms of nations and states only but in terms of human lives also? So I was reading one of your articles on the individual and imagined communities and where you wrote that the "Hindus", they were not a monolith. They were divided by caste firstly, also by language and region. So when you say that a Hindu from the North is similar to a Hindu of the South or a Brahmin of the South, this is a very fluid description. I think that a Brahmin of the North will have some similarities with the people of the North; but he will have much less in common with a Brahmin of the South. He will not be very happy with that comparison with a Brahmin of South. That's caste and also language. So people across ancient times were also divided in terms of language also. So it will be a very monocausal explanation to say that 'fine you share the same culture as me and therefore we're alike'.

Rustom Bharucha: Did you have a question about early India? Yes, please get to the question on early India.

Novojit Sen: So I'm saying that in early India, can we say that people of the same language, people who were from the same culture, same region, they were also divided by their economic conditions, divided by their material interests which were in fact placed opposite to each other?

Rustom Bharucha: Would you take the other question also? Yes could we take the next question? Okay fine. Sojendra?

Sojendra Mukherjee: Ma'am, I would just like to ask since we're talking about boundaries, whether the boundaries in ancient India are not shaped by the contemporary present-day politics? So in that way, the present is reflected in the past. Can we say it like that?

Romila Thapar: Which boundaries are you referring to? The boundaries of present-day India would not be shaping the past because the boundaries of present-day India are dependent on present-day politics.

Sojendra Mukherjee: No ma'am, boundaries not of present-day India. We're discussing about, say, India. When we're studying early India, we have a particular geography in mind. So that particular geography, does it not shift with our present understanding of India?

Romila Thapar: Geography, I see. Well obviously some elements of the geography would be shaped by what exists because after all geography is tangible. The mountains, rivers, deserts, plains and seas—these are all there. Although there has been some change of river courses, it's not been all that dramatic as to make a difference to the geography, although it affects human settlement. So that aspect of geography is important, yes. But if you're talking about how people visualized their geography, that's another story. If you're talking about how, for example, in ancient India, people talked about 'Jambudweep' or 'Bharatvarsha', that is a concept. That is a concept, part geographical and part cosmological. They were not describing these places on the basis of actually travelling around with survey equipment such as thedolites and making notes about what they saw. They were not noting the kind of rock formations, or which direction the river flowed, and so on. It was a concept. It was a concept of a universe in which a certain section was called Jambudvipa and another kind of demarcation was Bharatvarsha. This conceptual geography has very little to do with the actual geography that we refer to when we use the term geography today. The meaning has changed and you have to make a distinction between cosmology and geography. Today, we use the term geography which is based on data that is a different kind of data altogether from cosmology.

Rustom Bharucha: Yes. And what about the earlier question?

Romila Thapar: Well I think there were—as there are now, although slowly vanishing—regional differences based precisely on the characteristics that you mentioned, i.e. language, caste, religious beliefs and economy. The same existed in the past; but do remember that when one uses these categories, one must be aware of the fact that they play themselves out in a different way. For example, if you take a language like Prakrit, which was the language of almost the entire subcontinent except for the extreme south, which was Tamil-speaking, you can map from the Ashokan inscriptions what the sub-dialects were at the time. There was the main Prakrit that was used by many and then there were the dialects; and the major dialects are mentioned by Panini such as Magadhi, Ardhamagadhi, Shauraseni and so on. The major differences of dialect were for example, in Eastern Indian Magadhi where the 'r' sound was replaced by the 'l' sound. So in the edicts that Ashoka issued those recorded in the region of Magadha and Eastern India, refer to him as *'laja'* and not *'raja'*. That's one dialectical difference. In the Western Indian section—Ujjaini Prakrit—there are certain other differences like double consonants. The script of the inscriptions in the North-West is influenced by Aramaic which is the language used in Iran and Afghanistan at that time. So when you say that there are linguistic differences or language is creating an identity, you must be clear that you're not just referring to Prakrit but you're referring to a particular category of Prakrit.

Similarly, with caste. Yes by about 1000-1100 AD or so, every region of India had caste society and we know of its pattern from regional language sources as well. But the interesting thing is the difference in the way the castes were patterned. In the Punjab for example, at that time the Brahmins were not the dominant caste. They had a few land holdings and their status and role is characteristically different from other regions. In Punjab and Sind, the dominant castes were those of the traders. The Khatris were the dominant caste in the Punjab and the more numeous other castes included the Shudras. So there were Khatris and a small pocket of Brahmins, and a number of Shudra castes and then the still lower castes and the Dalits. That was the pattern in the Punjab. In Tamil Nadu at the same time around 1100 AD, the pattern was different as the dominant caste was the Brahmin. It was dominant not merely because of the *varna* system, but because the Brahmins controlled the land and the economy. They were major landowners having given large grants of land. Many of them were also major traders. Some of the big trading guilds like the 'Ayyavole-500', were from Brahmin *agraharas*.

So the dominant caste was the Brahmin and there were also categories of rich peasants, the *Vellalar*. Beyond these, there were all the lesser traders, merchants and artisans, and the Shudra castes and those lower down the social scale. So yes, one generalizes and says that one common feature in all the regions of India is caste, but do remember that when you look at caste, it may be wiser—if I may say so—not to do what some DNA specialists do these days. They pick up samples and grade them according to present-day *varna* castes—Brahmin, Kshatriya, Vaishya and Shudra—and project the results back in time, without going into the history of these castes to see when they acquired the status they are claiming, or what the pattern of caste may have been in the specific region.

In many of the regions, the actual pattern was different. This difference comes through lived experience. But colonial and nationalist historiographies have assumed that the actual pattern was identical all over. The historiography of the last 30-40 years, and recent social history is now showing that the patterns were different. So we are asking the question, as to why were they different? It is quite similar to the way we view religion. What do I mean when I say that 'one really can't talk about Hinduism as a monolithic category'? Remember, where does this label "Hindu" come from? It comes from Arab and Persian references to the people who lived beyond the border of the Indus, as Hindu/Hindi since the land was called al-Hind. It was based on the Iranian word Hindush and the Greek word Indos, for the river Sindhu. So al-Hind gives you the clue that the people who live in al-Hind are "Hindi" or "Hindu" and they use the two words interchangeably. Somewhat later, in about the $14^{th}/15^{th}$ centuries the term is extended to mean all those people who live in al-Hind but are not Muslims.

"Hindu" in its original meaning, included everybody whether Syrian Christians or Parsis or Buddhist or Jainas or

Vaishnavas, Shaivas, Shaktas or any other sect. They were all "Hindus" because they were not Muslims and lived in al-Hind. The question one has to ask is that if this term "Hindu" in a religious and not just a geographical sense gains currency in let's say, the 14th century, how did people whom we today describe as Hindus, describe themselves earlier? They must have used some label because we're all absolutely committed to labelling ourselves, we're constantly saying 'I'm this; I'm that, I'm the other. So the only thing one can do is to go to the sources where we find that the reference is to religious sects. They refer to Vaishnavas, Shaivas and Shaktas and they refer to the Shramanas who are Buddhist and Jaina. References to religious groups occur in two recognized streams that of the Brahmanas and that of the Shramanas. They are sometimes abusive about the other and sometimes complimentary.

What I'm trying to say is that when you use the category of religion, don't just say this was a region that was given over to Hinduism. You have to refer to the religious sects that were dominant, and not all these sects were equally dominant. In Kashmir for example, Kalhana's *Rajatarangini,* seems to suggest that the Shaiva was more dominant than the Vaishnava sect. So do remember that when you're dealing with the society of that period—early India—these categories have to be much more carefully worked out. And one of the problems with early Indian history is that we continue to use these blanket terms that were bestowed on us by colonial scholarship, and some of which was followed by nationalist historians. We have to investigate these categories much more rigorously and precisely. That is what I meant by the fact that whatever the boundaries may be, when you look at a region, you really have to put it under a microscope and break down your categories into many multiple categories, and then judge what the region looks like.

Rustom Bharucha: That's a very rich answer and it's full of subtlety. I think the danger when we're talking of this dynamic of the ancient and the present—oddly enough everything's become rigid in the present it seems to me. The categories are becoming more congealed. So for example, the category of "Muslim" got invented at a certain point in time and census reports for example, played a huge role in enumerating certain categories. Whereas in my work in Rajasthan when I work with musicians like the Langas and Manganiars, yes they are "Muslims" but what kind of Muslim is this? So I was very happy to hear you highlight the primacy of sects because we tend to shun that kind of word. We say 'oh sects, that's "sectarian", but of course that's the reality. There are different variations and gradations. Okay, let's now go to—Baisakhi, are you ready with your question?

Baisakhi Sengupta: Ma'am, what I want to ask is this: with every source that we read in early India or any other kind of history, we come up with a new perspective and a new way of looking at things. So as a history student now, I have a lot of confusion in my mind regarding what might have actually happened because there are so many kinds of interpretations that we come across. I was wondering if history is really about interpretations of different kinds.

Romila Thapar: Well, let me begin to answer your question by saying that most historians would also concede that there can be confusion in their minds about understanding early India. The purpose of research into the past is to clarify this confusion. There are no certainties about the past. That's the first thing you have to learn as a historian and I learnt it the hard way because I remember when I wrote my thesis on Ashoka, I happily made definitive statements; it was this, it was that, one reads it this way and so on; and my supervisor, Professor Basham, would keep putting little question marks and saying, are you sure? And I would re-read the texts and say no I'm not sure, and to this day I am not absolutely sure. Every time I make a statement about the past, at the back of my mind is the thought, 'that's what the evidence suggests.' But no one can be a hundred percent certain about the past. One can't even be a hundred percent certain about the present. When an event occurs today, at this minute, it's a *Rashomon* situation; there might be six different versions of what happened, from six witnesses. Therefore, if everything in life is that momentary and uncertain, when you're dealing with the past that is substantially an abstraction, then how can there be absolute surety?

The historian is therefore not concerned with discovering the truth about what happened in the past but with providing a rational, logical explanation and an understanding of what happened in the past, to the extent that it can be reconstructed from the evidence that we have. Ultimately, the past is an abstraction, a very important abstraction and it is not altogether disconnected with having some impact in formulating the present, giving direction to the present. But it is nevertheless an abstraction. Therefore, one cannot know the definitive answer about the past but can provide a reasoned and logical explanation using the clues provided by the evidence.

But keep in mind the fact that there are two things that constantly make history change. One is new evidence, which for the ancient period is hard to come by. So we don't have to worry too much about new documents being discovered and completely changing our imaginary of those times ; but change also comes when new questions are asked of the same evidence. New questions might force you to realize that your source is not just a single document but it could include three other documents that had missed your attention which you now realize are linked to the source that you're studying. In archaeology for instance, new excavations bring to light new evidence sometimes through discovery and sometimes through new questions. A paleo-pathologist may examine a few skeletons and discover that they were struck by disease, as happened some time ago with material from Mohenjo-daro. So the theory of the city having been hit by invaders had to be reconsidered. This theory was in turn revised when there was evidence of deforestation and environmental changes. So remember that in the same way that you cannot be absolutely certain about the past, you also have to keep in mind that you don't know when another kind of question might be asked which would lead you to reconsider the certainty with which you have proclaimed what happened in the past. So your confusion is a very good sign. Go on being confused.

Rustom Bharucha: That's a beautiful answer, I have to say. Just let's hold on to this in the spirit of the workshop when Romila

Thapar says, with her lucidity and clarity that is absolutely unmatchable, 'there are no certainties of the past.' That's an extraordinary admission coming from somebody who works with that much clarity. It's coming not out of a false kind of modesty, no, there are no certainties. It's very scientific, there's a certain kind of nuance to this. For example, in the post-modern kind of literary canon, indeterminacy has been overly valourised, but there's a different kind of indeterminacy being suggested here which is far more grounded. It's grounded in determinacy. That I find very instructive, and very very refreshing.

Romila Thapar: Talking about post-modernism, I'm constantly being asked that post-modernists maintain that every explanation has equal validity, so do I agree with this. My answer is that I don't accept such a position. I think explanations do have priorities, and to that extent the indeterminacy does not justify one saying that it is uncertain and therefore everybody's right. No, everybody isn't right. I'm more right than you or you're more right than me. I may have to chew my words and go back and admit that you were more right than I am if the evidence comes up that suggests this. But at the moment, given the uncertainty, I still have a sense of this is more right than that. Okay?

Rustom Bharucha: That's a very judicious kind of intervention. It's very reflexive, it's responsive and it's not anything goes. That's the problem when "anything goes" becomes a way of looking. That's just unacceptable to me at any level. I just find it irresponsible. When she uses the word—that's what it "suggests"—that word "suggests," is very interesting because there again that's a literary kind of category—the power of suggestion. You know what I mean, but that's also what a historian has to do. I think in an earlier conversation I said 'what do you do about this?' I was talking about Zoroastrian history, I'm a Parsi and what do we know about our past? So she said with great clarity, 'sometimes you have to guess.' The word "guess" is also not something you necessarily associate with the arsenal of the historian.

Okay, we're going to move into methodology now. I'm going to offer the time for the questions by two people. One is a question on objectivity; I mean that's one of the key words. It's by Swatilekha Bhattacharya from the School of International Studies. Swatilekha where are you? Ah, there you are Swatilekha, and there's another question, we'll just link two. There's Saumya Saloni who's an MA candidate in the Department of Sociology at South Asian University, and you're going to talk about—it refers at some level to genealogy, right? So could we begin with you Swatilekha?

Swatilekha Bhattacharya: Actually my question is a very basic one. What counts as history or as a historical event or as historical evidence? Because in academics we see a regionalization and nationalization of particular thoughts and this creates a bias in the things that we study, in the way we are being trained as academicians. So what is it that we take as categories of thought and as valid sources for evidence?

Rustom Bharucha: Could you raise you question?

Saumya Saloni: My question is about the work of modern historians in contemporary times. They are engaged in finding out reasons for particular events in history, and as we know *Itihas Puranas,* form the main constituents of genealogy, myth and historical narratives. So in order to preserve the records, they keep checking and rechecking these, and in a way this gives the sense that it leads to trimming of records. So how justified is it to limit the scaling of interpretation by pruning the records?

Romila Thapar: The simple answer is, that history is a narrative of what happened in the past. The more complex answer is, how do you know that this is the correct narrative? That is where the historian runs into trouble. I can keep on saying that my narrative is correct for this or that reason, and this is my evidence. Somebody else may turn around and say that your narrative is wrong, mine is correct. And when I ask for what reasons and evidence, the reply is simply that mine is correct. Such controversies are known on historical issues, especially when those who are not professional historians contest the views of those who are. History has developed a method of research and of analysing evidence and being a historian requires training. This was not the case fifty years ago. So it is difficult to convince members of the public that one cannot just read a few books and become a historian as one has to be trained to analyse sources. We've been through such controversies, some of us more scorchingly than others in the last 30-40 years, when we've been trying to say that history has to be much more rational, logical and rigorous in how data is analysed. Some people would use the word "scientific." And if one uses the word "scientific," in its simplest sense, I would go along with it, but if you use it as scientists use it, there may be problems with the historical method. Nevertheless, the question is that you define history in a way by defining the method that you use to arrive at history. The method therefore has to have a clarity of purpose.

I would suggest that one starts off with a question about the past. That question should be posed in a manner which is not just about the life of a person from the past or something of this kind. We now go beyond the lives of kings and ministers and try and gather information on the lives of other people as well. The question needs to be posed much more in terms of what were the practices, let us say, of a particular caste or occupation or how did they relate to others. You then look at the evidence and as a good historian should—all of us don't always do that—you look at the evidence and you test its reliability. The first question you ask is whether the evidence is reliable. There are various methods of testing reliability. I won't go into that because it depends on the category of evidence you're using. How you test a coin is very different from how you test the reliability of a text, but you must be sure that you know that either category is reliable.

Okay, the next step is that you ask yourself whether you have consulted all the possible evidence on the subject you are investigating. That is, having gone through the evidence, is there anything more that should be consulted ? This is a step that is very often missed out and it's a bit sad because it doesn't give completeness to the research that is being done.

Let me try and illustrate this. We use, for example, in our studies particularly of the first millennium AD (certainly earlier as well but more so the first millennium AD) inscriptional evidence. That is, inscriptions which are statements that are written up on temple walls, on other structures, on pillars, rock surfaces and on metal copper plates. Let us take for example some of the inscriptions of the post-Gupta period, recording that king 'X' belonging to this dynasty, whose other members consisted of 'A, B, C, D, E and F' has made a donation, and the donation consists of a certain plot of land which he has given to a learned Brahmin for performing a particular ritual to avoid the evil effects of an eclipse of the sun. The plot of land is indicated by its location in a particular village, its demarcation by a grove of sacred trees to the north, a pond to the south, a river to the east and fields to the west. The rights and obligations of the grantee are given: the Brahmin grantee can collect a stipulated revenue from certain persons and by collecting certain products from designated places and people, he has obligations in return, and so on and so forth. Then at the end there is a statement saying, that the statement in the inscription was dictated by the king to such and such scribe, who then had it engraved by so and so and the order is dated by a precise date which may be the equivalent for example, of January 8, 879. These kinds of inscriptions were found and read in the late 19th century by scholars who worked on Sanskrit, on Philology and on Indian history.

Right through that century and until the 1960s—that's almost a hundred years—the information that historians took from these inscriptions related to chronology and dynastic history. Who was the king? What was his dynasty? What are we told about the other kings of that dynasty? Who did he fight battles against and where? He married a princess and made an alliance, and so on and so forth. There was information about the dynasty, and the date of the inscription? So there was a collection of data on kings, their dynasties, where they stood in relation to other kings of the dynasty and their dates. The chronology of Indian history of that time was based on these inscriptions and practically every dynasty and many kings had issued inscriptions. So if you take all those inscriptions and put them in a chronological order, and you start reading the inscriptions from beginning to end, you'll get a history of that dynasty. Or, more accurately, something approaching a history of that dynasty.

This was it. And historians went on working with this until the 1960s when the question was raised whether these grants of land by kings to Brahmins and others created a system of political economy and land relations that was similar to what is called feudalism in Europe ? Feudalism was a European concept. Why did it come into Indian history? This led to the investigation of what these grants of land actually are. This in turn led to a collection of data on what was called economic history—land survey, the crops that were grown, the taxes that were collected, the rights and duties of the grantee and the relationship of the grantee to the peasant who was cultivating the land. Was this the parallel of the vassal and the serf and the feudal lord? Was this a European-type manorial system? Was it what Marx had called the Feudal Mode of Production? This debate went on right through from 1970 to the 1990s.

The notion of feudalism in India was first suggested by Indian Marxist historians, and the critique of its application to Indian data was also first made by other Indian Marxist historians. Some of these debates were held at the Centre for Historical Studies in JNU as we were interested in the debate and in alternate analyses of this period, a subject researched by many of my colleagues. As historians we realized that these inscriptions which we had taken to contain only data on chronology and dynastic history had a flood of data on economic and social history where castes were described and duties of castes were described, as also were religious sects and various other aspects of history. So there was a fresh appraisal of the same texts with a different kind of history being written.

Recently, some of us who have been working on historiography—the history of historical writing—are going back to the smaller sections in these inscriptions that are called *prashastis,* eulogies in praise of a dynasty. We have been examining the genealogies and statements on the dynasty from these *prashastis* as possible segments of a historical tradition, or of its core? So for a hundred years, historians looked for one kind of data from this body of texts and in the next fifty years they are suddenly flooded with a different kind of data. It is very important to realize that when questions change, the answers can also change and new aspects can be opned up by the new questions. If there hadn't been that question on what was the economic relationship between the king, the grantee and the peasant cultivator, we would perhaps not have discussed the theory of feudalism and of social and economic relations. And if we hadn't looked at the *prashastis* from the point of view of looking at the *Itihasa-Purana* or historical tradition, we would not have recognized the patterns in these genealogies. So please remember that history has to change as and when new evidence is discovered or new questions are asked. If a historian is asking a new question then the question has to be defended as a legitimate one. Is this a relevant question that can be asked of this data? In what way does it further the investigation? Let it not worry you if there are changes taking place because this is inevitable. To use a cliché, knowledge only advances if you question it, and if you discard existing knowledge when it is superseded by fresh knowledge. This is something that you really have to keep in mind all the time.

Okay, the genealogies—as part of the *Itihasa-Purana.* My interest in the Puranic data is with a section of the *Vishnu Purana* which has been called the *vamsha-anucharita*, the path of succession. It's a very interesting piece of information, being an entire section in the text that claims to be a kind of history. It begins with the beginning of the world when mythical Manus ruled for many years, each reign running into hundreds of years. Then came the great flood, everything was flooded and the seventh Manu was told by Vishnu to build a boat, put all the creatures into that boat, as well as the Vedic texts, and that he, Vishnu in his Matsya incarnation, would take the boat through the waters and place it on dry land. We have Noah and the ark being repeated here as well as earlier Mesopotamian myths. Then when the flood recedes, Manu comes back and becomes the ancestor to the two major lineages, the Lunar lineage of the Chandravamsha, and the Solar lineage of the Suryavamsha. The lists of these lineages are all given in detail and are claimed to be authentic as is the claim for all such lists. At the end of each, they fade out after a major war. The Suryavamsha through Rama, who fights a battle against Ravana and defeats him, but after this the lineage fades out. The Chandravamsha lineages are all tied together in the *Mahabharata* story. They're all battling against each other at Kurukshetra and after the Kurukshetra war is over, these lineages also begin to fade out. References to them are made and some dynasties claim descent from them but such claims are made some centuries later.

So I'm arguing that war is another time-marker like the flood. The flood covers everything, erases everything and out of it a history emerges; that history goes on and on through the descents and then a war ends that system. Then the text goes on and states that the author of the text will predict what is going to happen. It proceeds to list many of the dynasties that ruled up to the Gupta period, and these dynasties are attested by inscriptions. So the future tense becomes another time-marker. They're not writing it at the time of the Kurukshetra war, they're writing it in the Gupta period; otherwise they wouldn't have got the dynasties right. So we know exactly when that text was written.

The point about genealogies is, that they are central to the *Itihasa-Purana* tradition as attempts to remember what is thought to be the past. There may be a disagreement about my interpretation being correct but this is a part of my recent book, *The Past Before Us*, and I'm waiting for a reaction from scholars and historians. So why are genealogies so important? They are important first of all as time-markers. The word that is used is a giveaway, it's '*vamsha*'. This the name for bamboo or cane. Why is it a giveaway? Because the bamboo has a node, and then there's a stem, then there's a node and then there's a stem. So each generation is a node and the stem is connecting the generations. Okay? So genealogy is first of all a time-marker. It's a time-marker in a lineal fashion; it's linear, it's not cyclic. The cosmological time in the Puranic texts is cyclic—the *Mahayuga*, the four *yugas*—the *krita*, the *treta*, the *dvapara* and the *kaliyuga*. These are all cyclic ages, but the genealogy that is a fragment of the last of the four *yugas*, is linear. The role that is played by genealogy, not only by genealogy in the *Puranas* but genealogy anywhere in this world, is that if I want to say today that I am somebody of high status, one of the ways in which I do it is, that I get a genealogist to link me up with a high status ancestry. This would be done through a genealogical connection and people are encouraged to overlook the fact that it is fabricated. In the post-Gupta period particularly and after the *vamsha-anucharita* section has come to an end, rulers claimed to be of Kshatriya descent and got themselves linked to one of the two lineages or even invented a third. If a Brahmin provides the link it becomes more credible and possibly some were remunerated with grants of land for doing so. Once the Kshatriya claim is accepted it enables the newly established family to marry the daughter of 'X' who may be an old established Kshatriya family and marriage alliances were part of diplomacy. So genealogies are absolutely crucial in establishing status, social history and political legitimacy. That's why I take them seriously as a system of status but not literally as recording facts.

Rustom Bharucha: Wonderful answers. Has there ever been an occasion where you've actually been sceptical or you haven't trusted inscriptional evidence?

Romila Thapar: Yes, two occasions. One is the inscription itself. There appeared on the market, a stone slab with a fragment of a so-called Asokan inscription said to have been found in Northern Afghanistan. This was a new area that could be added to the Mauryan Empire so it made news. But some of us examined the inscription and felt that it was not genuine and could be a fake. There were also a couple of eminent palaeographers and epigraphists who thought likewise. So one has to make sure it's a genuine inscription. It's not enough just to be able to read the inscription, but you have to understand epigraphy and palaeography—the actual script can also give a clue as to whether it's genuine or not. That's one way of assessing an inscription.

The other is to check whether it follows the formula that commonly determines the framework of an inscription. Each segment of the inscription has some formulaic devices. It begins with a benediction, such as *'om namah shivaya,'* or its something similar and this gives the sectarian affiliation of the author. Then there is the *prashasti* where the dynasty and the ruling king is praised : the ruling king may belong to the Chalukya dynasty and the Chalukyas were great, they swallowed up all the oceans and subsequent to that there was a mighty ancestor and his deeds and those of his successors are listed. In the recording of the kind of grant being made it is necessary to state all the details, and these also sometimes have formulaic passages. I mean it's like the shorthand of the bureaucracy of the Government of India. When you go there and you say, what has happened to my file? And they say, 'oh your file? Yes yes, it is under due consideration', and you know immediately that "under due consideration" means it's forgotten, it's been put aside. So you have these administrative phrases. What happens sometimes in a fake inscription, the phrases get mixed up or they leave out a crucial word, and then one is suspicious about its authenticity until proved otherwise. Sometimes you do have inscriptions which make a statement—a brief statement possibly—and it doesn't somehow sound right. There's something there, and so you put it in with a question mark and you keep waiting to see if other evidence supports it. If you can get other evidence to support it, then that gives it greater authenticity.

Rustom Bharucha: It's very juridical.

Romila Thapar: It's very juridical. Yes.

Rustom Bharucha: You have to test everything out. The Langas and the Manganiars in Rajasthan for instance. There are many resonances of what you're saying. Well, they are genealogists. They maintain the genealogy of different kinds of patrons. Now genealogies can just be ridden-up? Like they can, in a sense, elevate social status?

Romila Thapar: They can elevate social status. But it's a question of how seriously you take it. I think in the old days they were taken much more seriously than they are now. But even to this day, I remember that when we took my father's ashes to Hardwar, and I was apprehensive about getting it right because

I'd never done this before, and I said to my aged aunt how would we find the right priest? And she said there would be no problem if I went to the centre of Hardwar and stood around looking lost, somebody would come and ask what I wanted and if I said I'm looking for my family priest, and name my family, caste and town. That is what I did. And within half an hour the *panda,* the priest who administered to our family and caste was there, holding the red book, the *bahi,* under his arm. He performed the required rituals, then took us to a little guesthouse, sat us down, opened the *bahi* and said he would now bring it up to date. So we filled him up on the names that were missing from his genealogy of the family. I teased him a little and asked how he was sure that we were telling him the truth. And prompt came his reply that he would of course cross check our information with the genealogical *bahis* kept by other priests who serviced the families into which our family had married. I must confess that I was quite impressed with this system of collecting, checking and retrieving data on family history. Now that is the point that in the old days, the genealogies of families from dominant castes were maintained at places of pilgrimage and these were visited when ceremonies were required at birth or marriage or death. In the winter these *pandas* used to come down to the plains and live briefly with the families to whom they had been allotted and update and cross check the information. Then they would cross check it with other people and make sure that what they had recorded was reliable information.

I could easily have said to the *panda* at Hardwar that I got married to the Raja of wherever and this that and the other. I could have made up a story about myself, he wouldn't quite have known till he had checked with another person who was holding the genealogies may be of the Raja of wherever or of families of a similar status. It's not only status; but in our kind of lives—a few generations ago—marriages were arranged through genealogists. If you were stuck, you couldn't find the right bridegroom for your daughter, and she was turning 17, 18, 19. What would you do? You would go to the genealogist and enquire whether there was an appropriate young man available for marriage and of the right caste and family. In some places the genealogist also recorded ownership of property or arrangement for the division of property in a family. Such records were acceptable in courts of law. So socially, the genealogist was a very important person in those times.

Rustom Bharucha: Very interesting parallels between this very down-to-earth method of verification, authentication and updating. Komal Kothari was full of these stories. Manoj Kumar, you had a question on the risk of creating fake history? Manoj where are you? Would you like to ask that question now or has Professor Thapar already raised the issue of fake history? Why don't you raise your question? Manoj you're an MA candidate in the Department of Sociology at South Asian University.

Manoj Kumar: With reference to *Ancient Indian Social History* (1978), I wish to ask as to how the transition from one kind of textbook to another took place? Was there a confrontation between champions of the two kinds of histories? Is there also a risk of creating fake history due to a certain type of historiography as mentioned by Hugh Trevor Roper's account of Scottish Highlanders' history in an edited volume by Eric Hobsbawm et al., *The Invention of Tradition*?

Rustom Bharucha: You had raised a question here, that's why I asked you Manoj. That's fine. Is there also a risk of creating fake history through the invention of tradition? That kind of thing. Thanks Manoj.

Romila Thapar: Well the one thing you must remember is that history as narrative is an old activity. It goes back to very early periods. Every society had narratives about its past, and some regarded them as history as time went on; others perhaps not consciously but certainly subconsciously thought the same. The one thing you must remember about the past is that it is very delicate in terms of what present politics can do to it. That is the biggest danger that the past faces—that present politics can completely disfigure the past. In a sense, throw acid on the face of the past. Keeping that in mind, one begins to understand that if the past is to legitimize the present, particularly if it is to legitimize politics, then this becomes a very crucial issue. Why does it do this? Very briefly, let me suggest that nationalism of any kind, anywhere in the world, whether it was European nationalism or Asian nationalism, does require history. Eric Hobsbawm has a passage where he says history is to nationalism as the poppy is to the heroin addict.

You cannot have nationalism without resort to history. And it introduces into that history its own requirements, such as what nationalism calls the period of a "golden age" when everything was utopian. It's usually the earliest period because that is the period when the evidence is scant and it's difficult to check its reliability so fantasy can overrule it if that is what is wished for. Utopian conditions can be more easily created. What happened in India was that first there was a colonial interpretation of Indian history which was largely geared towards colonial policy. That is where the Hindu-Muslim-British periodization was introduced because there had to be two communities in conflict with each other. This was essential to colonial policy. Nationalism picked up this idea and converted the Hindu period into the "golden age". Interestingly this also coincided with many historians of ancient/Hindu India being of the upper castes. A certain natural affinity was associated with this age. This was picked up by religious extremism. The Hindu Mahasabha, and later the RSS, the BJP and the Sangh Parivar, all project the notion that the Hindu period is the utopian period, and they carry their history forward with that. This results in two versions of history: the straightforward nationalist version which was the more secular version because it came out of a situation where the enemy was the colonial power and "we Indians" included everybody—Hindus, Muslims, Christians, Sikhs, everybody, all the castes, all the religions, all the languages and our shared history. The other was the limited history of the particular community aspiring to power. So it was we Hindus and our Hindu history, or else it was we Muslims and our Islamic history.

Nationalism finally wins with the creation of the nation-state and the colonial power is removed. Where is the enemy now? If the nation needs an enemy, and this of course is not a necessity but a choice, such an enemy has to be from within itself, and preferably your rival who succeeded in creating the other nation-state. And the other nation-state looks upon you as the enemy that resisted this creation. Democracy actually works far more effectively if there is no concept of an enemy within. But if there are aspirants for power with a religious ideology then democracy also goes for a six. What had started off as a germ in colonial policy, that the Hindus and Muslims were always antagonistic, now becomes a theory of history. And if Hindu nationalism has to compete with Muslim nationalism then it must have superior antecedents. So Hindu nationalism insists on the superior Aryan foundation of Indian culture. In 19th century Europe, the Aryan race was regarded as the superior race, and the Aryans were regarded as foundational to culture. So these two features—the Aryan foundations and the Hindu-Muslim antagonism became crucial to this particular kind of history.

Mainstream historians in the 1960s started questioning this construction based on colonial history and the demands of religious nationalism. They argued that the early beginnings were not utopian. They were like other societies and had their their ups and downs. They had positive features, they had negative features, and the Hindu-Muslim relationship was also uneven. Nor was this the only relationship that had historical consequences. Inter-community relationships could sometimes be harmonious and in other situations not so. Since situations varied they needed to be discussed and easy generalizations of one kind or another to cover all periods of history were not feasible. So this was upsetting the political apple-cart of using history to legitimize the conversion of the Indian state into one that gave primacy to Hindus as citizens. The ultimate vision of Hindu nationalism, was and is, a kind of Hindu state/Hindu Rashtra. There is a Muslim state in Pakistan. The counterpart had to be a Hindu state in India or something approaching that. So history is being used to justify the intention. The stalwarts of this history, people like Savarkar and Golwalkar argued that the primary citizen of India is the Hindu because India is his "pitribhumi" and his "punyabhumi"—the land of his ancestors and the land of his religion, and all else are foreigners. Therefore, if you're creating a state in which the Hindu is the primary citizen, you have to have a history that backs it up. The idea that it could be a secular state has little place in this vision.

So now it is being said that the inhabitants of India even in about 3000 BC were Aryan; the Harappans were also Aryans as was their culture. Many historians consider the Harappan culture and cities to be non-Aryan and especially so if it's essential urbanization and artefacts are compared with what we have from Vedic sources that were the texts of the Aryan speakers. DNA analyses are now being drawn upon to prove the ethnic identity of the people whom we know about from archaeology. We have to constantly remind people that Aryan is a linguistic and cultural label and not a biological one, whereas DNA has to do with genetics. The two cannot be confused.

Textbooks that should contain generally accepted information are unfortunately also brought into this debate. Textbooks which should be under the control of educational bodies and academia are, in this country, under the control of government—the Ministry of Human Resource Development. As long as they're under the control of the government, every time the government changes the history textbooks are changed. Last time it was only history; but in the last few years there's been an attack on social sciences as well. Now that the party in power has changed, the social science textbooks will change to support the ideology of this party. How does one stop that? One cannot, except by demanding that textbooks in all subjects should be the responsibility of professional teachers and scholars from the various disciplines with the required training. The vetting of textbooks should not be in the hands of government bureaucrats and diktats in this matter by quasi-political or religious organizations is particularly uncalled for in a state that calls itself secular.

Rustom Bharucha: I think so. Very interesting complexities for South Asian University where they have to deal with more than one government coming into power. So there are multiple governments with multiple readings of histories, multiple affirmations of histories. Very interesting to see how that gets negotiated. The next two questions are on authenticity, and I'm going to first ask Saroj Kumar Nepal who's an MA candidate in Sociology at South Asian University. Saroj where are you? Okay and there's another question that's coming from Slok Gyawali, MA candidate from Department of International Relations, also at South Asian University. He wants to talk about authentic history vs. imposed history. So will we begin with Saroj?

Saroj Kumar Nepal: If there are alternate or conflicting narratives explaining a historical event or personality, how does one establish the authenticity of which narrative ensuring that it is 'true' and 'correct' and not imposed on the historian or fabricated by those in power?

Rustam Bharucha: Okay and what is the second question, Slok?

Slok Gyawali: My curiosity is along the line that history will always be a controversial discipline. Because it is interlinked with politics, the difference between "authentic history" versus "imposed history" becomes important. Additionally, history is also subject to what the historian, or more generally, the custodian of narratives, decide to leave out. Add to this, the notion that "fact is like a sack" and the entire endeavour seems problematic. Considering this, how can history as a discipline be useful in addressing contemporary issues, especially as a "linear sense of time" collapses? I'd be interested in learning what Professor Thapar thinks about the conclusiveness of a historian's idea of the past, and its impact on the present.

Romila Thapar: Okay. Where are we going now? I wish I knew. I wish I could say this is where we're going. I really have no clear idea. After 2004 some of us historians who wrote the textbooks were at least, released from being abused every day in parliament by spokesmen of the NDA–I government. This I must say was a relief. In 2005 I did write and a couple of others also wrote many articles in the press, saying that the National Council of Education Research and Training—which brings out the textbooks—should be converted into an autonomous statutory body. It should not be under government control but under the control of the professional teachers who know the disciplines. Have a committee or a body which is elected every two or three years or whatever it may be, and make it their responsibility to vet the quality of the textbooks that are used in schools. We went on writing this and some of us even appeared on TV channels and explained why it was necessary, but as you know our views were ignored.

Nothing has been done; nothing at all. And I know perfectly well that nothing will be done because it is a politically powerful weapon for a political party to have textbooks, especially social science textbooks, in its hands and under its control. You can give education a political direction by putting in anything from garbage to really excellent content, but chosen for political reasons. I think education in this country has been deliberately neglected because the politicians are frightened of an educated electorate. So I think the textbooks will continue to be under government control. The HRD Ministry is already threatening to change and revise the social science textbooks. If the Gujarat model is any indication of the nature of change, then I'm afraid the future looks bleak. The answer to your question is, 'let's see what the next election does and the kind of government that comes in.' The kind of government that comes in will determine what kind of social science textbooks we'll have. It's a very cynical answer I know, but I'm afraid I think it is probably the right answer. But to move to the next question ... Sorry, just remind me again, I'm getting old.

Rustom Bharucha: Imposed history and authentic history.

Romila Thapar: Imposed history and authentic history. What do you mean by authentic and imposed?

Slok Gyawali: I actually came across this in an interview I saw of yours. In the *Hardtalk* interview with Karan Thapar, you talk about authentic history and imposed history.

Romila Thapar: Oh, I think it was in the context probably of the textbooks where I was arguing that the historian's history is likely to be more authentic history. Let me just say that as we're talking about authentic history and in relation to my answer to an earlier question about the lack of definitive conclusion in history, it's not as if history wanders around floating without any conclusions. We do have conclusions, and they are ordered in priority. The point that I was making was not that there are no conclusions, but that conclusions can change, although only after serious analysis—not just to support political propaganda or the whims of those in power. And this is a point which I think is now conceded even in scientific disciplines, particularly after Kuhn's book on the nature of scientific revolution. It's perfectly well-understood that as you get more information, conclusions change and the same happens with the asking of new questions. So that's all I meant; I wasn't suggesting that we go around saying, 'I don't know.' I do say I do know, but I have to always add, 'I do know in the context of the information that we have at the moment'. If it changes, then of course one reconsiders. So by authentic history, I was meaning the history that is written by historians, that is read by historians, that is reviewed by historians and that goes through the process of being sieved by one's peers and one's professionals. Imposed history is precisely the opposite. The government produces a textbook and dictates what is history and insists that everyone has to agree with what is said.

In a sense I am asking myself what prompted me to write textbooks for schools. The first lot of NCERT (National Council of Educational Research and Training) textbooks were those that I wrote for middle schools; for 12 and 13 year olds. I wrote *Ancient India* and *Medieval India*, and although initially I was applauded but later I was criticized by a few friends and more so by critics for being a statist and for subscribing to the state system by agreeing to write the books? It's very difficult to explain why one agrees. I agreed in 1963 because I was still an unquestioning nationalist and I thought this was an important cause, and the existing school textbooks were so bad that it was unfair on a generation of children not to expose them to a richer history and an understanding of the past. I'd been through the ones used in Delhi schools, and they were really dreadful, and I thought that it was something that we had to change, in order to give education some quality. In the next decade other historians also agreed to write textbooks.

But what I mean by imposed history really was the kind of history that is not accepted by historians, nevertheless, it is imposed in schools or, even at the level of universities an attempt is made to bring in a uniform syllabus for all universities—something that was being attempted by NDA–I and has been revived by NDA–II. That would also be an imposed history since it is expected of universities by definition to have autonomy in working out their syllabi. By extension I might add that authentic history is a history that even if it is not written by a professional historian is acceptable to the latter to the point that historians will defend it. The imposed history is what a political ideology or a government wishes to have taught.

Rustom Bharucha: You know sometimes the categories almost seem to collapse on other political contexts, and I'm thinking of Rwanda where we of course know there was this terrible genocide. Now history teaching has been, sort of, suspended. No history is taught in schools because they have to figure out their history. It's a very very momentous moment when we can think about it because the primary ethnic categories of Hutu and Tutsi have been outlawed. So you cannot legally refer to yourself as either Hutu or Tutsi. But how do you deny the past? This is, I say, a bit of a conflation because the government obviously wants a new history. So it's going ahead with the sanction of the government; but it is being put together by a whole battery of historians including historians from Berkeley and other places. So it's a professional kind of historian who would be involved, but what's the outcome? We don't really know. Okay, we'll have to move on to a somewhat different question and we're still working through methodology. Renny Thomas is a research scholar in the Centre for the Study of Social Systems at JNU. Renny where are you? You're a sociologist Renny, and what is your question for Professor Thapar?

Renny Thomas: As a sociologist I am interested in the question of the present and the interpretation of the past. Prof. Thapar's essay on Weber and Durkheim, and the one on secularism needs to be mentioned here; my intent is to compare and contrast with the way sociologists and anthropologists see the past and interpret sociological discourse. How scholars like Weber and Durkheim pursue the idea of Indian society through their historical writings—How can we use fiction as a way of writing history?

Rustom Bharucha: I'd like to just add, since he brought in fiction Romila, the question on *Sakuntala*. So the question on Sakuntala was asked by, I think, Adithyam. Where's Adithyam? M. R. Adithyam from the Department of History? Is Adithyam here? It's okay. So anyway but it's a question I thought that could be linked—the different ways you can draw on different narrative modes.

Romila Thapar: Well this little essay that I did on Durkheim and Weber, that was really the outcome of just generally looking at how some European scholars looked at India at that time. I was worried that it was not based on extensive reading and I may have been wrong because I haven't studied sociology or social anthropology as such. Whereas sociologists would look at people like that from the past in terms of what was their contribution to the discipline, or how did they give direction to the discipline? I think when an interloper like me comes in as a historian, my interest is much more in the extent to which they reflect the historical background from which they have come, using India as the object of study? I think my interest is really historiographical. That would be a fundamental difference between the way a sociologist would look at their work and the way in which a historian would look at their work, although it is by no means the only difference.

Yes, now on the question of fiction. Today what is happening is that in some ways we're going back to the 18th century when there was great excitement because it was said that every subject has a history; history is fundamental. So everywhere you went, whether you were a geologist or whether you were a plant specialist or whatever, you started off by looking at the history of the discipline. Now I think in some ways, we are coming back to that kind of thinking but from a slightly different perspective which is that everything that the historian looks at is also to get an idea of the background from which a particular text emerged. So in that way, the historian touches on all kinds of texts which needn't be historical *per se*. And fiction, I think, is a very important area in which a historian can move and work. Fiction in earlier times was always treated by historians as largely only a source of information. You could pull out little nuggets of information from a text especially for early Indian history where there weren't straightforward histories, but always remembering that it was largely fictional, it was literature. We would say, it says such and such in a Kalidasa play, and this can be used as information or as incidental evidence. Then what happens is that the historian, broadens the perspective and says that fiction if it is a product of an age and of a genre tied to an age, it's telling you something about the age.

That was the argument with which I started when I did my study of Sakuntala. My point was, that this is a fictional story but it is repeated through the ages in different forms. So first, why is the story important? Why is it constantly repeated? And secondly, are the different forms telling us about the age in which each version was written? So you have Sakuntala in the epic tradition; she comes out of the story in the *Mahabharata*, which is different from the story in the way Kalidasa presents it as a play, which is again different from the way in which it is presented in *Braj Bhasha* as a kind of local folk drama. So there are these three, different ways of presentation. My argument was that in each of these, what we're really gathering as historians is what can be said about the society that is the context to each version. Is it describing clan society in the *Mahabharata*? Is it projecting the notion of kingship and patriarchy in Kalidasa? Is it describing the local small town society of 18th century India in the *Braj Bhasha* version? Okay? Then one goes on to consider the translations. There's an English translation and there's a German translation. The German poets all think she is magnificent and endorse the way in which she is projected. They call Sakuntala "nature's child".

Then the English Orientalists regard it as good for reading and learning Sanskrit, but they introduce for the first time, an objection to what they regard as its eroticism and they say it's too erotic for an English audience. They delete what they think are the erotic passages from Kalidasa's play, and then allow it to be used as a college textbook. This is a different take again and the take draws on Victorian eroticism. Then come the two essays of Tagore who discusses the Kalidasa play as reflecting initially the physical and subsequently the spiritual in the relationship between Sakuntala and the king. In the first part of the play, Sakuntala is a fallen woman, and he uses the term "fallen" (*patita*), and at the end of the play she has been through the *tapasya*/ascetcism of separation and she has emerged as a spiritual being, she has become spiritualized as it were. I was fascinated by the fact that one could take something that was completely fictional and yet read it through these different perspectives of varying historical periods and see how they represent attitudes to women. So in a sense, the historian is in a very fortunate position that she can take up any aspect, any kind of literature and attempt to read it as a statement about that time.

Rustom Bharucha: What role does aesthetics have to play in the historical investigation of a fictional text?

Romila Thapar: Oh it has a major role. Yes. The more I have thought about it since doing the book, the more I see the diversity of the presentation. I think the epic version is really straight, to-the-bone absolutely bare. Kalidasa is just beautiful in terms of language. Here the historian does have to make that concession that it is a text that is not staying with the bare skeleton of the story as in the epic, but introduces a frill of aestheticism and that is important.

Rustom Bharucha: When I directed *Sakuntala*—just an interesting casting of *Sakuntala*. I cast a Siddi woman as Sakuntala. She just happened to be in with the group of people I was working with in a rural area of Karnataka—Siddi person of African origin, and she indeed has grown up in a forest. She is, in a sense, a forest woman. While I was working on the play—it's a different process from that of a historian—it became absolutely clear to me while working in the play that this is a reworking of the Sita myth. It just becomes very palpable. Now of course there are the conventions of Kalidasa where Sakuntala has to go back to her husband. In fact, Sakuntala almost disappears and she's unimportant. She kind of fades away, while in my production she couldn't, and that's where interpretation enters. She in a sense had to return to the earth. It became very interesting to see how going back to the ancient and the present, how in theatre there's a different dynamic because that ancient text once it gets embodied and enacted is in the present.

We're going to move on to *Somanatha* and I'm going to kick it off with a methodological question and then move into the more, kind of, ideological questions. Pragya? Where's Pragya? Is Pragya here? She's not come? Well I'll just read out her question: "My question is methodological with reference to the works of Professor Romila Thapar such as *Somanatha: The Many Voices of a History* wherein she uses multivocality and multilingualism, use of Persian chronicles, Jain biographies, Sanskrit inscriptions and colonial and nationalist histories with a wide range and close-up perspective. Professor Thapar arrives at a diverse and differentiated historiography which allows for a more fluid and dynamic understanding of social group formation. I request Professor Thapar to deliberate on this methodological issue." This issue of *Somanatha* I'd just like to link it to other questions on *Somanatha* and they both come one after the other. Yes, Krishna Pandey? Is Krishna Pandey here? Krishna Pandey is an MPhil/PhD candidate in Sociology at South Asian University. You have one particular question on *Somanatha.* Why don't you ask your question then Krishna on Somanatha? And we can link it to the earlier question on multivocality.

Krishna Pandey: With reference to the seminal work *Somanatha: The Many Voices of a History*, Prof. Thapar argues that the raid on Somanatha temple by Mahmud of Ghazni in 1026 AD and other such subsequent events do not have a communal basis and therefore nothing to do with Hindu sense of trauma. This has led to some resentment among Hindus and political rightists as she was seen as interpreting the incident only as an effort of gaining control over temple properties with full economic motives but not with any religious or communal dispositions. *Somanatha: Many Voices* is an effort to challenge the monolithic interpretation of Hindu-Muslim interface in South Asia but, at the same time, the question is still unanswered whether these interfaces could only be looked at from Marxian specs.

Rustom Bharucha: Are you trying to say that in dealing with this destruction, that there are many other readings and other interpretations that don't have to be seen in the context of iconoclasm or a kind of communal history or religious history or economic? What are you trying? Try and sharpen your question.

Krishna Pandey: For example, a single historical event may have different sources. Sometimes there will be different historians who are working on different evidences and because of different historians working on different evidences, perhaps there will be different conclusions or different interpretations. So for different conclusions either the students are responsible or multiple evidences are responsible.

Rustom Bharucha: Who's responsible for multiple interpretations?

Romila Thapar: Well there's a simple answer to that question. Historians are responsible for the interpretations because they're the ones who're interpreting it. The evidence doesn't speak by itself. The historian has to make the evidence speak and so what one's listening to is the historian making the evidence speak. But on this question of multiple sources, multiple voices, I'll mention two things: one, I've already referred to as the practice of not using Sanskrit sources extensively after AD 1000 because of conforming to the old periodization. That fortunately has been done away with now. So we can carry on using Sanskrit sources even when we move into the second millennium AD. When an event has been made into such a crucial event of the present as Mahmud's raid on the temple of Somanatha, the historian has to go into the question of trying to ascertain how different people at the time saw it. That is precisely what I tried to do in this book. The basic question is what are the sources that we have that reflect opinions about the event, or comment on it, or even make no comments about the event, although they refer to that period of history when the event took place? Or for that matter, even sources of later periods that look back at the event or just at the places and peoples of that area. That was one reason.

The other was of course ascertaining the validity of the major comment that is constantly referred to in modern times which is tied into this question of whether Mahmud's raid created a trauma among the Hindus of such dramatic proportions that it seeded a permanent hostility against the Muslims. This "Hindu trauma" is often mentioned from the late 19th century. This has been made much of in modern history as well as politics. Ideologies of resentment against the Muslims on the part of Hindus are explained by the trauma suffered by Hindus after the raid of Mahmud of Ghazni. I thought this was an important enough question to be investigated. So the investigation went as follows: I first of all looked, very carefully, at all the Persian and Turkish sources, some of which were written soon after the raid, and some much later. These are the sources that are always quoted on this subject. For a historian, the immediate and crucial question is that of when were these texts written? How soon or how late after the raid? Most accounts were written much later. So there is an interesting range of descriptions of the object/icon that was destroyed, and the reason for it being destroyed. Let me give you just two examples of how different it is. In one Persian text, it says the icon was a stone representing the image of Goddess Manat, who was a pre-Islamic, Arabian goddess, and Muhammad had said that Manat had to be destroyed together with two other goddesses but this image had been secreted away from Arabia and brought to Gujarat and it was kept in the temple of Somanatha.

That is one version of the image in the temple which occurs quite soon after the raid. It's not a Hindu image at all. There's another version which occurs about 600 years after the raid in a Persian text which says that the icon, perhaps a *lingam* was made of metal, and there was a magnet that hung above it so that the icon was drawn to the magnet, and it was suspended between the floor and the ceiling. Obviously an awesome site, where the image is actually like Trishanku, it is in the middle between earth and heaven. I looked at these two descriptions and wondered at the fantasy. But there are other references also quite fanciful of Mahmud destroying a Hindu image. Sometimes it is a lingam, sometimes it is an image with a head, sometimes it's an image with a body and when they strike the stomach of the image, precious stones fall out. I thought that's a bit strange because stone and metal, when struck cannot produce precious stones from the belly. So one is left with the feeling that the reconstruction of that act is a fantasy reconstruction. Every author that had an idea about how he wanted to reconstruct it, did so, and wrote it up as a story. Now I have no doubt that Mahmud did come and that he did destroy the icon which was a lingam because there is one sane, sober account which is the earliest account and that is of Al-Biruni. He said Mahmud destroyed the icon that was placed in the temple and describes it as a *lingam*.

Then we turn to the Jaina accounts. They tell us that the Shaiva temple at Somanatha fell into disrepair. The Jaina chronicle of Merutunga was written well after the raid of Mahmud but refers to events concerning the temple a couple of centuries after the raid. So it's not a very long time after and if there was a Hindu trauma, it would be remembered very precisely and reported by the Jaina authors. The latter were learned scholars by the way; Hemachandra and Merutunga are amongst the best Jaina scholars in a highly scholarly tradition. Merutunga writes that the temple was in a state of disrepair because of two reasons: because it was on the shore of the sea the salt spray kept hitting it which had worn away the lower level of the temple and that wicked ministers had not maintained it properly.

So Kumarapala, the Chalukya king, was told by his minister that if he really wanted to gain renown, he should repair the temple. So Kumarapala rebuilds the temple. There is a lovely description in the Jaina text of its consecration. The king takes Hemachandra, who is his minister and is a Jaina, along with him to the temple for the consecration ceremony. Kumarapala then turns to Hemachandra and asks for proof that Jainism is superior to Shaivism. That there was a rivalry between the Jainas and the Shaivas at the time is hinted at in other sources. And Hemachandra turns to the image of Shiva which is a lingam and prays to the deity to manifest himself. There's a powerful white light and Shiva appears before Kumarapala. The king is so impressed that he immediately becomes a Jaina and gives up drinking alcohol and eating meat and observes all the vows. That is a Jaina chronicle of the Chalukya dynasty written in Sanskrit and therefore neglected by earlier historians because for them the sources for the Muslim/medieval period were in Persian.

Then there are a large number of Sanskrit inscriptions. Some were issued before the raid of Mahmud and these state that pilgrims come often to the temple at Somanatha bringing offerings and money. But the local rajas of the region, and among them the Chavdas are mentioned, loot the pilgrims. The Chaulukya kings have to organize the defence of the pilgrims against the local rajas. This is before Mahmud comes. Then the raid of Mahmud takes place, but there is no reference to it in the inscriptions as indeed there was none in the Jaina chronicle. The next important inscription is the one issued by the chief priest of the temple, Bhava Brihaspati, who claims to belong to a great lineage of priests from Kanauj and he states that his ancestors were appointed chief priests of the temple. He claims further that he had persuaded Kumarapala to restore the temple to its glory. Kumarapala did so. There is no mention of Hemachandra or the Jaina tradition perhaps because he is a Shaiva. Curiously neither the Jaina nor the Shaiva authors record the destruction of the temple or that it was converted into a mosque. They simply say the temple was in disrepair and it was then repaired and functioned normally again. So that is another version of the story.

Among inscriptions there is a very interesting one written about a couple of centuries after the raid of Mahmud. This is soon after the Bhava Brihaspati inscription which records the renovation of the temple. This inscription is bilingual in Sanskrit and Arabic and inscribed on stone. It was issued by a Persian sea-captain called Nurud-din Feroze or as he's described in Sanskrit as Piroja. Nurud-din Feroze states that he has trade relations with people at Somanatha and that he wished to build a mosque so that those who accompany him, the sailors and the artisans, would have a place to pray. He says he appealed to the local raja, Phoolchand, and he agreed to give some land for building a mosque. The local council of Somanatha consisting of all the *thakurs* and the *rajas*, the representatives of the traders and the representatives of the artisans' guilds also decided to give him land from the estates of the Somanatha temple. Reading this inscription I said to myself, here's a horse-trader from Persia by the name of Nurud-din Feroze. He obviously comes often to Somanatha where he has trading connections with local traders and he asks for a piece of land from the local raja who then speaks to the trading corporation as it were, and the trading corporation agrees to give him land some of which is from the estates of the Somanatha temple. Obviously by now it was a very rich temple again. The mosque is referred to as a "dharmasthana" which incidentally is a word that is sometimes used for temples as well—a place where you worship. Then the story goes on in more Sanskrit inscriptions.

A successor to Bhava Brihaspati who was the chief priest of the temple, obviously a very sharp witted man called Tripurantaka claims that he has had many temples built, and he's on the committee that looks after the temple of Somanatha. He has close trading relationships with traders from Persia, bringing in horses to India. The horse trade was a highly lucrative trade along the west coast of India from Gujarat down to Vijayanagar and Goa. So I began to say to myself, if there was a Hindu trauma, surely these respectable members of the Somanatha elite wouldn't be trading with Muslim traders and giving them land to build a mosque. Therefore what does a trauma mean? One would expect that if there was a trauma and that the Hindus were deeply upset by the raid on their religious place of worship, that they would distance themselves from the persons associated with the trauma, i.e. the Muslims, since it was one of them who had caused the trauma, and such persons would be treated with contempt. Here what is happening is that whether they were deeply upset or not, they were not distancing themselves from the Muslim traders. They were cooperating with them, building their own trade through this cooperation and giving them a piece of land from the estates of the sacred temple of Somanatha for them to build their place of worship. Far from a trauma, it is really an act of cooperation and friendship.

Anyway, this goes on and there are other references to the temple as a place of worship at least until the reign of Akbar. Other Persian texts however state that up to the 15th century, some armies of the Sultans of Delhi claim to have raided the temple and converted it into a mosque. The temple is again in a state of disrepair and they put a dome on the top of one part of it. It's not demolished, it's still there, but they claim that it has been converted into a mosque. And every Sultan's general who comes to Somanatha after this claims to have attacked the temple and converted it into a mosque. One has to ask, how can the temple be demolished and then converted into a mosque each time. The temple built by Kumarapala continued although in a dilapidated condition until 1950. That is when it was fully demolished and a new temple constructed on the site in 1951.

But prior to this the British also contributed to the story. They had been doing badly in the Afghan wars and suffering deep humility. At this point Lord Ellenborough, who was then the Governor General, ordered the commander in Afghanistan, Lord North, to bring back the gates of Mahmud's mausoleum because he maintained that they were the gates of the Somanatha temple. Where he got this idea from no one knows. North brought back the gates from the tomb of Mahmud in Ghazni. When examined it was discovered that they were not Indian but probably Egyptian. They had nothing Indian about them. So obviously Mahmud didn't take any gates from Somanatha. This action of Ellenborough raised a debate in the British House of Commons and members began to question Ellenborough's motives. Was he trying to please the Hindus by bringing back these gates ? It certainly made the British look rather foolish. In the course of the debate one member of Parliament tried to defend Ellenborough by stating that he was probably trying to assuage the trauma of the Hindus who must have been absolutely traumatized by the attack of Mahmud of Ghazni. This appears to have been the starting point of references to the trauma of the Hindus. I have found no reference in any of the sources to the trauma of the Hindus prior to this debate in the House of Commons in 1842.

Anyway, the debate carries on and a century later India is declared independent. Soon after this, K.M. Munshi, the Minister of Education in the independent government demanded the rebuilding of the Somanatha temple. (Incidentally, he also founded later in the 1960s, the Vishwa Hindu Parishad, so his background on these matters is evident). He made the rebuilding of the temple a matter of Hindu pride and wrote to Nehru, demanding that the Government of India do so. Nehru promptly wrote to say that the Government of India was a secular government, building neither temples nor mosques. He added that if Munshi wished to rebuild the temple he would have to do it by setting up a private trust to finance the rebuilding. So they set up a private trust to build a new temple. They removed most of the old temple and replaced it with the new one. The Archaeological Survey of India objected strongly to the destruction of a protected monument but it was over-ruled. But the new one was built exactly where the old one has stood. Pieces of the old temple were moved into an adjoining space and labelled as a museum.

The more recent continuation of the story is well-known as the Rath Yatra of L.K. Advani. It was said that he was avenging the insult of Mahmud of Ghazni raiding the temple of Somanatha, which had led to a Hindu trauma. So the event had to be avenged even though this was being done a thousand years after the event. That is the story of Somanatha. The problem however is that if you listen to the multiple voices, there will be contradictions because the voices are saying different things. Each one is proclaiming its own importance. The Jaina chronicle is saying that we are the important people, we convinced Kumarapala to patronize Jainism and the incident is narrated that marks the occasion. Bhava Brihaspti is saying that the king was a Shaiva and the temple was built because we told him that he has to do so. The Persian chroniclers are trying to outdo each other in stating that Mahmud was so great that he destroyed the temple, the icon and he killed both infidels and Shias in exggeratedly large numbers. Now this is a case where the historian has to assess the reliability of the evidence being used. This was not done to the extent that it should have been, by earlier historians. They tended to use much of this data at face value.

First of all, they did not analyse the Persian evidence as being perhaps make-believe to some degree because they thought court chronicles are generally truthful. Now we all know that every chronicle that is written in this world, whether it is European or Persian or Chinese or Indian, has a substantial element of untruth because it is written for a purpose: it's propaganda for the ruling king so it's bound to be exaggerated in part. What needs to be done is to analyse the Persian chronicles and see why they are exaggerating and what they are exaggerating and where these lovely fantasies come from. I was fascinated with the idea of a huge magnet and a large iron *lingam* being lifted by this magnet, and I asked myself where at that time were scientists talking about magnets and iron? And sure enough, there are some rare references to this but entirely unconnected to Somanatha. May be we should explore the theories current in places such as Baghdad which were centres of scientific discovery at that time. These are the interesting themes that historians should be investigating. Earlier historians did not compare the Sanskrit texts with the inscriptions or with the Persian sources or try and correlate them.

Let me return to what I said right at the beginning about the link between the past and the present: The past is the past but the British were trying to use that past to legitimize their present, and so how did they use it? They used it in the fashion described above and their version of the past comes apart today because they were obviously making superficial generalizations. The fantasy of bringing back the gates of Somanatha, led to the debate in the British Parliament and this resulted in their story of the Hindu trauma. K.M. Munshi, who had his own political ambitions picked up the notion of the Hindu trauma and made much of it. His book on Somanatha is not without echoes of the debate in the House of Commons, with some phrases based on that debate. Now of course the issue has become—as your questions demonstrate—very much part of the present. I am asked why I am trying to whitewash Mahmud. And I have to say I'm not whitewashing Mahmud. I don't approve of people going around bashing up idols and destroying temples and pulling down mosques, and that kind of thing. But I'm trying to understand the event and trace the subsequent story since I am convinced as a historian that the popular version about the history of Somanatha does not reflect what actually happened in the past. I don't claim to be narrating the correct version of what happened over those many centuries, but my reconstruction makes more sense to me than the ones that preceded it. I'm putting it together from all these different versions and saying that this is the way in which I arrive at this proposition today.

Rustom Bharucha: Thank you. Thank you, that's an amazing exposition. I think we're very privileged to have this kind of articulation of a process. I mean she's written the book but my god, when you hear it; it's a very rich education I think for all of us. I mean what work has gone into this when you really think about it. How much work has gone into reading these different sources, collating these different sources but also reading against the grain in a sense; reading with scepticism, not trusting everything. I think this came through more powerfully here than in the earlier part. This really was somebody using common sense, that's what I find humorous. There's a lot of common sense here. How could it be this if they're doing horse trading here and they're giving the horse trade a line? It doesn't make sense that he's going to be traumatized. It's really hugely problematic how traumas get invented and that's all over the place. There's an invasion that takes place in the past, it took place a thousand years ago, like my forefathers came from Persia and Iran. What is the myth? The myth is that we were thrown out by those Muslims. Which Muslims? Were they Muslims? Who were they? And then that becomes a kind of nodal point in our imaginary and it plays out in very very problematic ways. So history becomes a corrective; it's not saying I have the right answer but it's trying to complicate the falsehoods and the manipulations that are taking place in the present.

We have three more questions, we've got to go fast because it's been long and I want to spare Professor Thapar more, she's really been generous with her time. Is Sudipta here? Sudipta Gorai from JNU? Sudipta you had a question on imagined religious communities and you were talking about the worshipping of the mother goddess and why is it so different in its practices from the dominant Hindu Brahmanic culture? I think could you raise your question now? You may ask your question.

Sudipta Gorai: My question is with reference to works such as *Imagined Religious Communities, Ancient History and the Modern Search for a Hindu Identity.* They offer arguments on "Hindu" traditions, iconography and rituals, and the fact of Saktism is traced to Harappa. Prof. Thapar writes, "The centrality of worshipping the goddess was initially new to upper caste religion. Some of these sects deliberately broke the essential taboos of Brahmanism relating to separate caste functions, commensality, rules of food and drink and sexual taboos". How then can we see the historicity of the worshipping of mother goddess and why is it so different in its practices from the dominant Hindu Brahmanic culture? While we try to relate the mainstream historical culture with the identity formation of individuals, will not the regional histories and mythologies of the specific place, to which the individual belongs, also be in a continuous interplay? When we talk about the history of India, are we not marginalizing regional histories? And also the history of the North-East? So is there any possible way that we can include these histories in our history books in school?

Rustom Bharucha: So the marginalized histories and histories of indigenous people, as we say, "tribals". I mean our language and nomenclature is quite problematic.

Romila Thapar: This is something that really belongs to more recent times because what is generally referred to these days as "history from below" only goes back to about 40 years although now there's much more of it. This is one case in which I think the nature of the evidence had imprisoned the historian because prior to this, we were so dependent on written texts and the validity of written texts that many historians rejected the oral

Image courtesy of South Asian University Archive

tradition. Few were willing to concede that as evidence. The change came with the recognition of the oral tradition as a source of evidence on the past. It is particularly important in association with history from below since written sources in the past were generally confined to elite groups who were literate. People lower down in society were generally not educated in literacy and therefore their articulation was largely oral. This was what I tried to do in the history of Somanatha where I included the narrative about Ghazi Miyan based on a folk tradition about this man who's supposed to be the nephew of Mahmud of Ghazni, and how integrated he is with today's Hindu society of Western Uttar Pradesh. But I must add that it requires training in the use of oral sources to be able to ensure the reliability of the evidence cited. Without this training a literal acceptance of the oral tradition could result in rather dubious historical generalizations.

So the historian is just beginning to reach out to other traditions, other kinds of evidence and the oral tradition is one of these. A major influence in conceding the importance ot the oral tradition has been the history of Africa. There has been much work done on the oral tradition of the history of Africa. The reconstruction of Bantu history, for example, is almost entirely based on the oral tradition, and it's been developed into a sophisticated method of using oral sources. So much so that I wouldn't dare look at an oral text and try and analyse it because I have not been trained to handle the methodology of the oral tradition. It is a methodology in itself. Once it comes to be applied to people who have not produced written texts but have an oral tradition, then their history will change, it is bound to change. But this is going to take some time because people have to be trained. I don't know that there is any Department of History in this country which is training historians in assessing oral sources. Yet it's crying out to be done.

Rustom Bharucha: You know, I have a direct response to that because the only thing I've ever written as history is an oral history as you know, drawn from conversations with Komal Kothari. I was at UCLA, making a presentation and there was a leading historian, let's say from India—I won't mention his name—massive pundit and knows several languages and so on. There was a very condescending attitude shown towards Komal Kothari's grasp of history, and indeed I know that my own book has been questioned on grounds—is it a history? And I think it's a fair question at some level, but the fact that you are open to orality, for example, you take genealogy and we take a mode of evidence like the Shubhraj which are the panegyric verses sung by Langas and Maganiar. You get dynasties over there that go back a long time. Now of course are they made up? Well all evidence is made up; no evidence is a pre-given. I think we have to know how to read that. That's the real test really, how do you read that orality? What are the things you have to be aware of in terms of tone, formula, etc.? Speed, pitch. I mean it's a very different art and you're quite right, I don't think we're training people for this. But I think maybe this is where the social sciences and something like the performing arts can come together because it's an embodied practice. So it's coming out from the voices and the bodies of particular people who are trained to go on for hours and hours narrating genealogies.

Romila Thapar: It is another method, and it needs to be looked at much more seriously than is being done.

Rustom Bharucha: So we've come to the last two questions and I could ask Quack Johannes, who is a Fellow at the Jawaharlal Institute of Advanced Studies, to raise his question? Is Johannes here? Yes please.

Quack Johannes: I have a question on Charvaka Lokayata. I was just wondering what happened to this tradition and whether you have any idea on how you could answer this?

Romila Thapar: Well, let me first of all say that it's not a tradition that I've worked on very much except in its earliest phases. The Charvakas are mentioned in the early stages of city-life and as contemporaries of the Buddha and Mahavira and more so in the Buddhist and Jaina texts. I find it extremely interesting that there is this tradition. What has interested me also is the fact that both ancient and modern commentators have tended to underplay it. So much so that modern commentators hardly refer to it. Histories of Indian philosophy generally have one chapter on the Charvaka tradition, if that. Yet, in some of the medieval texts, writing about contemporary philosophy of those times, there is a chapter on the Charvakas. So I suspect that it was very much there. It may have been treated as a kind of subterranean tradition which kept surfacing, which kept getting argued against, but was not given the publicity because there might have been a fear that this kind of thinking might become more powerful than it should be.

So there is a degree of hostility to it, certainly in Brahmanical texts. On the other hand, I'm not sure that we haven't in a sense, looked at the medieval period texts with this in mind, and that it might not be so hidden. In the same way as, for example, one speaks casually about the decline of Buddhism, that it just faded away and it is not very clear as to why this happened. But when looking at the structure of what is sometimes called Puranic Hinduism—the Hinduism of the first millennium AD and the period of the post-Gupta religious texts—there's much in it that they're obviously imitating from the Buddhist tradition. But it's not something that's been worked on sufficiently. So I think the Charvaka tradition is a very important tradition, and more so as it has not received the attention it deserves.

Rustom Bharucha: Could we end with Ankur's question? Ankur Datta teaches in the Department of Sociology, and he is raising a question related to the Babri Masjid which indeed was one of the big moments that really sparked a lot of thinking and rethinking on history and accountability. Yes Ankur?

Ankur Datta: You wrote about the kind of challenges that many historians like yourself face and how historians have to deal with these challenges—an absolutely political challenge. This was no longer purely academic. You were dealing with something that in many ways, for some scholars, may have affected their livelihood, the way you did and also it's a large moral challenge. That government's gone, and it's been about 10 years since. I was wondering at that time the challenges were clear. What are the challenges, if I may ask, that face historians, especially historians of India and historians in India now especially when a particular party or a well known figure might even come to power. The impact of neo-liberalism on universities, education and increase in privatized universities where disciplines like history are sometimes ignored, disciplines like sociology and social anthropology are made to fit a kind of convenient developmentalist model.

Rustom Bharucha: Thank you.

Romila Thapar: I think the challenge is even greater now. It hasn't gone away. And I say this because I think what has happened in the last 10-15 years is that the mindset of the middle class, certainly in this country, has become much more prone to accepting false history in the sense that there isn't nearly enough questioning of what is passed off as the popular understanding of our history. It has in part to do with middle-class aspirations over-riding the earlier demands of observing the validity of facts, because today it would seem that anything goes. The other reason is that the educational system has become so backward that students are not taught the difference between information and knowledge nor are they taught how to question information in oder to ascertain its veracity. They are merely taught to memorize their textbooks and regurgitate them for the exams—and the contents of most textbooks can only be described as utterly inferior. There is no attempt at the quality control of textbooks. This is really going to be quite frightening if, in fact, there is also going to be a political backing for what goes into textbooks. I mean its bad enough that it is the way it is. One can try and fight it at an academic level and through educational institutions, but if it comes to have political backing then we're talking about a different situation altogether. I think the mindset has got that way largely because—and here I'm being a pop-sociologist—largely because it is a society in turmoil, in transition in a much bigger way than we assume.

There's a certain superficial, surface modernization that deceives us. We start believing that because people dress in a particular way, talk in a particular way and behave in a particular way, this reflects a wellspring of seemingly modern thinking although it really does not. There is a return for instance, to what is imagined as tradition. It's again that invention of tradition which has been going on as part of this mindset which really has been quite destructive. The mindset is there, what's also making it much more effective is the neo-liberal economy where there is a situation today where unfortunately the only two things that matter in life are access to money and political reach. If you know the right people and if you have the money, you can get away with murder. This has contributed not only to corruption involving money but also the devaluing of morality. By morality I mean the intrinsic values of honesty, social justice and standing up for basic human rights. We don't have these as essential ethical values in our society any more. There aren't any rules because one knows that one can with impunity break any law one wishes to, provided one has money and can name the right people in one's defence.

So it is a society which is in a desperate condition; it's not just the fall of the rupee against the dollar that is doing this. In these kinds of conditions, one thinks of the Great Depression and thinks of what happened after that. It's these kinds of conditions in which false history has an appeal because it's easy, it's accessible, its one-sided, it's the history that doesn't tax one's powers of thinking, and it's emotionally satisfying since the past can be used to legitimize any practice that stems from the present. Consequently, I think that academically we may be very much better than we were 20 years ago, in the sense that 20 years ago probably such a large audience of people wouldn't have come to listen to me. But I think at the same time, as far as the larger society is concerned and eventually the kind of history one is writing and the history one is teaching, is tied into the society that one is referring to and coming from. The larger society is not really concerned with this kind of "authentic" history; it would much rather have the imposed history and just get away with that. So I'm sorry to end on such a pessimistic note, but there it is.

Nevertheless let me add that there is a silver lining. Perhaps in a few decades we may possibly get back to some reasoned, logical thinking motivating public opinion about the subjects on which we research and write and which we teach. I can say without hesitation that the advance in the writing of Indian history today makes some of it comparable to the best historical writing anywhere. Some of this is happening in Indian academic circles and some in universities outside India where South Asian history is taught. Attempts may well be made to silence this advance but these can only be temporary even if highly objectionable. As long as historians continue to adhere to a critical enquiry into their sources and into their reconstructions of the past, Indian history will remain worth studying and reading.

Rustom Bharucha: You know the role here of education, in a deep sense of the word not just academic, not just passing your exams or writing a good term paper which matters of course. But what matters more is the education about this larger society where we live in; it's massive. What are the kinds of tools that we need to bring to our own disciplines, admittedly in small ways, whereby these debates and this kind of—what I simply call—critical thinking, has to be really reinserted into the agenda. That's what I think we try to do in what we teach. If you can think, just think. And I thought today we had a very good example where a very experienced, seasoned historian laid bare her own process of thinking, I think, in an exceptionally honest way.

I think as I return to it, there's considerable labour in this process. Also, you have to be critically open. She's always saying it's not just quantification of material, it's not a simple matter of 'I'm going to get as much evidence as I can.' You need to of course create a pool of evidence, not just of one source, but you've also got to be able to know how to read it. That reading and that thinking goes with many other kinds of preparations politically. I don't mean political in a narrow sense but political in issues relating to justice, in relation to freedom and in relation to right, all of which seem to be steadily denuded in the kind of neo-liberal economy that has indeed infiltrated even the academia. So I think in some ways, the task today is greater than ever before.

I don't think I will even try and sum up what has been said. Let's look upon it as a process. Let's look upon this as processual. Let's look upon this as something that is simmering in your mind, maybe confusing you. Get out of this door and do something with it. It's not going to happen immediately but let it simmer, let it disturb you, let it confuse you. That is something that we must put our faith in. There are no easy answers here and if you had the easy answers, I'm not sure we'd be better off. It would be a kind of utopia that would be very terrifying and suffocating. I'm trying to say that it can be a catalyst for making you just a more thinking, reflective and hopefully a more caring human being. I think that's what the University has to do in all kinds of multiple ways. So I would just like to thank you for this amazing education. I certainly learnt a lot along the way. It was extremely lucid, very honest and very reflexive. The work that goes on in the life of the mind is huge. It's a huge, endless process. It just doesn't end. So thank you all for inviting us here and for being such an attentive audience. Thank you.

Now, may I request Saumya Saloni from the Department of Sociology to deliver the vote of thanks.

Saumya Saloni: This is indeed a very good and fulfilling afternoon, isn't it? I'm Saumya Saloni, a second year MA student in the Department of Sociology. It's my privilege to propose a vote of thanks on behalf of the Department of Sociology and Faculty of Social Sciences. With due humility, I must thank to begin with, our esteemed and august guests this afternoon, Professor Romila Thapar and Professor Rustom Bharucha. It was a pleasure for all of us to listen to such an engaging and enriching interaction. Your riveting intellectual persona will inspire us in our pursuits. Thank you so much ma'am for giving us this experience of a lifetime. I must mention our deep sense of gratitude to the Chair of the event, Professor Rustom Bharucha, who added qualitative value to the workshop. It requires a great deal of creativity and patience to chair an event of this nature. Thank you sir! What a dynamic participation in overwhelming numbers from various institutions based in Delhi. It was indeed a moment of 'wow' for us looking at the overwhelming participation. I sincerely thank you all for being significant flesh and blood in this workshop. I wish to express our sincere thanks to the President of our university, Professor G.K. Chadha, who has been a caring guardian of the family called South Asian University and who has been a source of constant support.

Nothing can happen overnight. The wheels started rolling months ago. I would like to thank Dr. Dev Pathak for his motivated and dedicated effort to conceptualize and coordinate the event. Thank you sir! Last but not the least, since no performance is possible without the backstage support, I would like to acknowledge the charismatic labour power of Mr. Samson George, Mr. Siddharth Jain and Mr. Aman Kumar. They always eagerly extend helping hands in organizing these kinds of events smoothly and successfully. Thanks abound to them. I would also like to thank Ms. Manori Bandara for logistical arrangements, Mr. Vineet Ghildyal, Mr. Aslam Ansari, housekeeping staff and the IT department for their constant support. On the successful conclusion of this event, I would like to request all of you to kindly proceed for refreshments. Thank you all once again.